A Boy in the Water

TOM GREGORY

PENGUIN BOOKS

PENGUIN BOOKS

UK | USA | Canada | Ireland | Australia
India | New Zealand | South Africa

Penguin Books is part of the Penguin Random House group of companies
whose addresses can be found at global.penguinrandomhouse.com.

Penguin
Random House
UK

First published by Particular Books 2018
Published in Penguin Books 2019
001

Set in 11.28/13.86 pt Dante MT Std
Typeset by Jouve (UK), Milton Keynes
Printed and bound in Great Britain by Clays Ltd, Elcograf S.p.A.

A CIP catalogue record for this book is available from the British Library

ISBN: 978–0–141–98875–7

For Rosie and Beatrice

The sea is calm tonight.
The tide is full, the moon lies fair
Upon the straits; on the French coast the light
Gleams and is gone; the cliffs of England stand,
Glimmering and vast, out in the tranquil bay

'Dover Beach' by Matthew Arnold

Contents

Prologue

4.30 a.m., 6 September 1988, Wissant Bay,
Northern France

John flashed the car headlights again. The seascape illuminated briefly as he did so, but no reply came back from the inky blackness. It was still very dark. The Vauxhall Cavalier was parked at the top of a slipway, beyond which a long sloping beach ran out to sea. From inside the car I could just hear the waves breaking on the sand in the distance; happily it was a soft, rhythmic sound rather than an angry one. To the right of the car a headland ran away out to sea on the north edge of the bay, while behind us, somewhere in the vicinity, a lighthouse flashed its occasional warning to the unseen shipping out in the Dover Strait. There was no one else around but the three of us in the car.

'Where the bloody hell is Willy?' asked John from the driver's seat.

'Don't worry, you know he'll be here,' replied Dennis from the passenger seat, after a long, nervous pause. The pair sat in silence – John anxiously repeating the headlight-flashing routine more than was probably necessary.

I was in the back seat, under strict orders to remain asleep, but was wide awake – had been since we rolled off the ferry at Calais two hours earlier. I had tried to sleep as the car wound its way out of the silent port town and into the countryside beyond and to the south. The sneaking glances I had caught from the car revealed a lowering crescent moon, on what was a clear and chilly night. Probably a neap tide given the moon. John said this meant 'less water' in the Channel. The trip over on the night ferry had shown me there was still plenty enough of it.

I quietly lifted my head to get a peek at the situation from the gap between the front seats. I caught another glimpse of the beach, and of the vast black English Channel that lay before us.

John jerked his head around. 'Tefal! How many times have I got to tell you? Go back to sleep!'

'I don't feel tired, John,' I pleaded. He didn't reply. Dennis offered John a sympathetic glance on my behalf, which might have said *Leave him alone, John – how would you be feeling?*, had it been accompanied by any words. But it wasn't, and John remained silent, so I gazed out, without further reprimand, into the blackness.

The beach ran for probably 50 metres beyond the slipway before it met the water's edge. The white flashes of the waves could now be seen as well as heard, but still, they were slight rather than angry. I judged from the state of the beach that we were probably at half tide, and that the water was on the ebb. I was facing westwards where the night sky was indistinguishable from the dark sea. Off in the distance, there were some occasional lights to be seen.

The lights came and went at random. Some flashing, some constant for a while, some with a green hue and some that were clearly red. Had to be shipping, I thought. John was fond of reminding me that this was the world's busiest shipping lane – presumably most ships preferred daylight given it didn't look *that* busy out there. Then they could see all the swimmers, like me. The chances of a collision or accident seemed remote. Besides, I knew we had a special blue and white flag to fly. For a moment I thought about how they would not be able to see the flag before the sun came up, but quickly decided to think of something else . . . ships were supposed to stay out the way, according to John, so that was all that mattered.

Off to the right I could suddenly see clearly a passenger ferry a couple of miles offshore, presumably bound, like me, for Dover. It was lit up in the darkness with its many decks and portholes visible. As it made its way out into the black sea I wondered if it was the same boat we had come across on from England just a few hours earlier.

I remembered the grumpy man in the ferry canteen who had loaded my plate full of fried breakfast during the night crossing. John always said that fried food was bad for swimming – bad on account of its ability to make you feel, and be, sick. It struck me now, a little late, that John had made me eat the biggest greasy breakfast *ever* on the way over, and with no explanation. The grumpy man just filled the plate with food, before repeating the procedure for the next person in the queue, which, apart from me, looked to be made up exclusively of truck drivers. I ate every mouthful of the fry-up, which tasted great, safe in the knowledge that I would need the calories. John and Dennis just watched on as I fed greedily – not eating, but sipping cups of tea. The three of us looked quite out of place compared with the truckers, none of whom spoke to each other, each sitting on their own.

Suddenly a much closer light appeared offshore – probably just 200 metres or so. A fishing boat, Willy's fishing boat. The boat, which didn't seem very big to me, was illuminated on its flat deck, and I could just about make out the shape of people moving around on board. There seemed to be a small wheelhouse at the front, behind which a roof of some kind covered the flat working area. It was bobbing up and down in the swell – accentuated by the fact that it looked to have come to a halt and was no longer carving its way across the blackness.

The boat looked very alone, with nothing else nearly as visible in the offing. John flashed the headlights once more, and this time the code was answered in kind by a search lamp on deck. A sudden sickness came over me. I had felt it before and knew what it was. It wasn't the fry-up. It was fear.

'OK. Let's go. Tefal, get changed,' said John. My heart thumped. I found myself gulping, trying to swallow a lump that had appeared in my throat on hearing John's instructions. I felt myself calm down after a couple of deep breaths, and a wave of childish excitement came over me, replacing the fear as it did so. John and Dennis got out of the car. Dennis went to the boot and started unpacking various bags and boxes. John rummaged around in his own kit bag – a very old-fashioned blue leather Adidas sports grip from another decade – looked at his watch, and briefly consulted a page of notes concealed within his trusty book-like clipboard. I had no idea what was written on its pages – John never let me read his notes, and even when I had tried (often) when he wasn't looking, his handwriting was worse than mine. I stood by the rear passenger door of the car, dropped my swimming bag on the slipway and began the familiar routine of getting changed in the open, with a towel to cover my modesty, even though it was pitch dark with not a person in sight apart from my companions.

As I stripped out of my cosy tracksuit I felt the cool air on my bare skin as the breeze coming off the land blew through me and out to sea. I put on my special trunks – the ones I had worn up at Windermere that summer, *and* the summer before – and tied the cord carefully. I reached in for my bright orange swimming cap and for my favourite pair of goggles. I had remembered to throw some talc into the inside of the cap when packing, so it came open easily as I pulled it onto my head. It was still quite new so had the full thickness, which could sometimes deteriorate over a year or more – not that this in any way contributed to keeping warm. The goggles – were they the right goggles? – yes, they had knots on the elastic on each side to stop them working loose over time, and this special pair had not one, but two knots in the right-hand strand. That's how I knew they were the special pair. The goggles were clear ones – John only allowed the clear ones. He said it was important to be able to see into a swimmer's eyes.

In a minute or so I was changed, my clothes shoved hurriedly back into my own kit bag. Facing out to sea, I stood still and silent in the breeze, in my trunks and orange hat, goggles in my hand, and waited for John.

'Come here, Tefal,' he said, and I joined him in the light provided by the now full-beam headlights. The surrounding world had become invisible as a result of the brightness – I wondered what the fishing boat was doing, along with everyone on board. Who even was on board, come to that?

'Dennis, pass the grease,' said John firmly, as he pulled on a pair of blue plastic medical gloves. Dennis handed him a pot from the top of the box of supplies that now lay at the front of the car in the glow of the beams. John opened the large round pot, forced his gloved hand inside and swore. 'Fuckin' 'ell!' Dennis turned with a quizzical look. 'This grease is bloody rock 'ard.' Under normal circumstances this would be a cause of great amusement: the swimmer forced to endure a cold application, which typically meant the removal of any body hair as the grease was worked onto the skin (although this was less of a problem for me on account of my age). But these were not normal circumstances. 'Get it in the footwell. Whack up the heating,' said John sharply. Dennis, who had just that moment lit a fag, did as he was told. John looked anxiously at his watch again. 'And gun the engine while you're at it. We'll start with the Vas instead.'

Vaseline, unlike the wool fat that was now under the heater, could be applied cold, and was thought to be better for those areas prone to salt friction – under the arms and between the legs. As John worked the Vaseline into and around my armpits in big lumps, I stood motionless, like a scarecrow, legs spread and my raised arms bent, in an 'M' shape, looking out to sea. No words were spoken for a while. Much of this routine had become a drill, so they weren't needed anyway.

John held out another fresh blue glove in the silence. I pushed in my hand, which was too small for the glove. He offered the tub of Vas and I took a large wad of the grease into my spread fingers. I worked it into and around my groin, paying particular attention to the lowest part between my balls and bum, where I knew the friction could get severe. No one ever enjoyed getting greased up. It was embarrassing, sometimes painful. I had long since given up believing that the grease helped my body to stay warm. After all, I had little doubt that the Brazilian swimmer who'd died of hypothermia just a few weeks ago on her attempt was well greased up. It felt like more of a ritual that, if nothing else, at least protected the skin against salt friction and the effects of long-term immersion.

We waited in silence for a while. John ordered up the wool fat from the footwell and, to my surprise, just a few minutes under the heater had done the trick. John went about his work. The grease was pliant and soft. 'That's a first,' I said, smiling. The first moment of attempted humour I could recall for many hours. There was no reply. Back, front, legs, and finally arms. A camera flash went off in the dark. Dennis, having smoked another fag, deployed his Instamatic and started to record events. The camera spool made a familiar clicking noise as he wound on the film, ready for the next exposure. It said something about the changing mood that he felt comfortable to take a picture. Behind the camera his face formed a knowing smile.

His own daughter, Alison (or Miss Piggy as she was known to me), had done this in 1983 and, for a matter of just hours, held the world record for the youngest girl to swim the Channel.

After a few minutes, and halfway through a fresh pot, the work was done.

'Now don't bloody touch yourself, Tefal, eh? And I don't care what you want to scratch.' I knew John wanted me to keep the grease off my hands, because if I didn't, it would eventually find a way onto my goggles, and if it did that, I was 'blind'. And that could make me lose the boat, especially once I became tired.

John reached back into the box of kit and pulled out something new. He unwrapped a foil tube containing a plastic light stick – the kind I had seen for sale before on Fireworks Night with Dad. They had chemicals inside that, once 'snapped' and allowed some air, would glow for hours, until the chemicals lost their magic.

'That's new,' I said.

'I know,' he replied, 'but I need to be able to find you in case you decide to swim off in the dark, Tefal.' I considered the point in silence and felt it unlikely that I would, but then I had never been swimming in the English Channel in the dark before. Especially not in the French bit.

'. . . and just for the record, Tefal,' he added, 'don't fuckin' do that. OK?' He demanded an answer.

'OK, John.'

The light stick snapped in John's hands, and immediately began to emit a faint green glow. John held it up, looking disappointed, but then, as if remembering forgotten instructions, shook the stick violently. Suddenly it became as bright as any torch. 'Hold that,' he said, as he reached for a length of twine in the box of kit. He threaded the twine into the stick's moulded plastic hole, before issuing the same instruction. 'Hold that.' I grabbed the green glow for a second time. This time a pen-knife was produced from the box. Having unfolded the blade John went behind me and grabbed the rim of my swimming trunks. After some fumbling from his chubby fingers, presumably to attach the twine to the now pierced trunks, he grabbed the stick and tied it on. I could feel its slight weight and wiggled my bum, looking anxiously at John as I did so.

'Don't worry, Tefal. It floats. You won't feel it once you're away.'

At that moment, I heard the buzz of an engine – quite a high-pitched, busy noise that I knew to be an outboard motor. A small boat, a tender – only a dinghy really – was working its way to shore. Behind it, the fishing boat lay in place, rocking in the swell. One of the people on the tender had a torch, which meant I could track it as it raced to the waterline, still some 50 metres away from me across the sand.

Dennis stubbed out another fag and, without words, walked over to John and patted him on the back. 'See you in Dover,' he said. John looked at him and, after a pause, and with a slight smile, said, 'Thanks for this, mate.' Then he turned to me.

'Right, Tefal, it's time. In a minute I want you to swim out and meet the boat. I'll be going across to the boat in the tender, so DON'T worry, but I'll need to go ahead quickly in front of you, so you can keep swimming once you get to us. You can't get fuckin' lost . . . just swim out to the big boat. It's the one with all the lights on,' he added with a note of sarcasm, coupled with affection.

'Got it,' I said, with all the confidence I could muster.

And I did get it. John and the others would need time to board the trawler, get their kit on board, and secure the tender before we were ready to move on, which was quite a palaver. I would be cold, swimming fast to warm up, not keen on hanging around.

'How're you feeling?'

'Nervous,' I replied, with a little more honesty this time.

'You'll be fine. Let's just get it done.'

And with that the conversation ended, and we walked down the dark beach, John with his trusty kit bag in hand. The tender was now ashore, half lodged on the gently sloping sand. Another flash went off behind me, as Dennis took another snap. I didn't look back.

The tender had a crew of two, neither of whom I recognized. The younger man was operating the boat, and by the time I got to the water's edge, was fiddling urgently with the outboard that had been tilted to allow access to the beach. Judging by the stopwatch around his neck I guessed the other man was the official observer, from the Channel Swimming Association. Both were dressed in cold weather gear with woollen hats on. It must have been a chilly night coming over from England.

John climbed into the tender, and the young man, who held it steady as John boarded, got more than just wet feet as he struggled to push the boat out to a floating depth. Having boarded himself, he ripped the outboard cord, which fired the engine, and I heard the clunk as the gear was engaged and some low revs moved them gently out to sea. From within the boat, now bobbing, in neutral again, and some 20 metres in front of me, John called out in a measured tone, 'When you're ready, Tefal.'

I brought my goggles up in front of me and looked at them. My heart knotted as I noticed that one of the plastic lenses had a good smear of white grease across the front. It must have brushed against my thigh as I walked down the beach. I knew that I'd made a mistake I might come to regret. But it was too late to do anything about it. I wasted no more time and pulled on the goggles. They felt familiar and comfortable.

Then I stepped into the water, ankle deep, and shook out my arms. The waves were still slight, breaking over my calves. My cold feet triggered familiar apprehension – the moment of full immersion was just seconds away. There was never a pleasant way to enter the cold sea. The water out in front appeared quite calm, but it was still dark and my eyes had yet to adjust. I had swum in much worse conditions at any rate. Would these conditions hold? What was it like beyond the shelter of the bay? The rolling of the fishing boat 200 metres or so away gave a clue that things might be different offshore.

So this was it. On the other side of the darkness somewhere in front of me was Dover, and England. I was going to swim there, on a route that would likely become a minimum of 28 miles on account of the tides. It was hard to know how long it would take. I'd only ever swum about half that distance but I thought up to fifteen hours was likely – double the time I had managed in cold water before.

If I could do all that, and it was a *mighty* 'if', I would hold a world record, because at that moment, I was eleven years and 333 days old.

1. *Changing Lanes*

5.45 a.m, 6 September 1988 – 30 minutes, 1 mile west-north-west of Wissant Bay, English Channel

I rose to the top of the swell just as the boat entered a trough and rolled back towards me. I looked down on the occupants of the boat. Someone on board was being sick, but from the water it was hard to know who as it was still dark. Another nice early problem to solve given I had time to occupy, lots of time. Probably the doctor or the photographer; it couldn't have been John, JC, Mother Duck or Spike, all of whose faces I had picked out on the neon-lit deck of the trawler in the first minute of being beside the boat. They were too accustomed to this kind of thing. All bar John had made their way over on the fishing boat overnight from England, I realized. I hadn't known who was going to be on the boat other than John himself and the doctor, I had assumed, so I felt a wave of euphoria as I realized each of them was there to help me through; it was like walking into a surprise birthday party but without being able to talk to friends, or say thanks.

Likewise, neither Willy the pilot nor his two sons, who collectively formed three-quarters of a fishing family from the famous shore fleet at Lydd, were likely to be the person being sick. Then I remembered that Dr Ian, conspicuous on the deck on account of his thick red beard, was a sailor, so concluded it had to be the photographer. I hadn't known there was going to be a photographer either, and so this had been the first puzzle – who was the stranger on the boat? He looked vaguely familiar from the distance at which I observed him. He was young, good looking and athletic, and probably in his mid-twenties. Perhaps he was a lifeguard with a hobby; he had been playing for quite a while with what looked like a fancy camera with large lenses, the sort you see at football matches. Maybe that's what made him sick – he should have been looking around him for the first hour at least, even in the dark. It was a 'swimming club fact' that focusing on the horizon was the best way to avoid sea-sickness. He was trying to stay out of sight, and to vomit on the other side from me. John Bullet, conspicuous in his trademark blue and white bobble hat, would have insisted on that. John would have been insisting on a lot of things at this point, some more important than others. There were watch routines to be established, tea to be made, notes to be compiled. This was a meticulous operation and he would have planned every last detail. As ever, my safety was in his hands, but also, on this occasion, in the hands of Willy the pilot. So much had changed between John and me in just four years, I reflected; but it had all started very differently, back in 1984.

My first trip to the swimming club in Eltham, aged seven, was not one I enjoyed. Mum made Anna and me go along one Wednesday night at the start of what promised to be a long summer holiday, claiming it was a good idea to try out new hobbies. I thought it a bad idea from the start. Not only was I nearly the slowest swimmer in Miss Morgan's school swimming lessons, but I could barely get across the width of the pool and had to stand up to rest halfway across. Besides, I didn't need another hobby – not with a new football sticker album due out any time now. I was very unhappy that the tales relayed by our cousins, Carolyn and Victoria, who had been members of the swimming club for years, had influenced Mum to take me. But this was just the latest tragedy in a year where I'd had to move house *and* start school, which meant spending less time in Greenwich Park or on Shooters Hill with Mum.

And Eltham Baths seemed huge to me. It had two pools – big and small – and in the summer the swimming club used only the small one for younger swimmers. Apparently the older swimmers were 'in cold water'. This had something to do with swimming in the sea, as both Carolyn and Victoria had told fanciful stories of swimming the English Channel with their swimming club friends. I'd been to France on a ferry myself, so I was doubtful as to how true any of this was. Girls did like to boast, after all.

The small pool was about the same size as the one at school but had no diving boards. Changing rooms surrounded it – single wooden cubicles, with a plastic curtain to hide behind – women on one side, men on the other. All around the poolside there were older kids, teenagers I thought, barking instructions at small groups of younger children, all of whom wore bright orange swimming hats. Some groups were swimming back and forth busily across the width. In other groups the kids hung onto the rail in a line, watching the bigger kids on the poolside, who were miming how to swim.

Anna and I were taken by Mum to a desk near the entrance, where a woman was signing people in – like a school register. On the table in front was a tin box full of money, and a list of names on a pad. Mum spoke to the lady, who did not appear to be all that friendly, and we were promptly told to get changed and 'to report' to the shallow end. This was *just* like being at school, I thought. And who wanted more of that?

Anna and I found a couple of spare cubicles, ignoring the men and women rules, and got changed. I had my school swimming trunks with me and a pair of big yellow swimming goggles that Mum had found for me in the toy shop in Blackheath. We walked to the shallow end where a grown-up was marshalling other children into groups. 'OK, who are you two?' she asked us. 'My name is Anna,' said my sister. 'And my name is Thomas,'

I added. 'Can you swim?' asked the adult. She was wearing a tracksuit and trainers, just like Miss Morgan.

'I can, well, sort of, but Thomas can't,' offered Anna for both of us. She often spoke for both of us. She was right, though. Swimming was at best an occasional activity for our family, but Anna could do a few lengths on her own. Whenever we all went swimming, I was much keener on diving in and floating to the top. Dad said this was brave, but even so I ought to try and swim more, and dive in less.

The grown-up sent Anna to one group of kids her own age, and me to another of the smallest kids of all. I felt anxious once we were split up as I'd expected we would stay together for the entire ordeal. I fought back the urge to cry as, for the next thirty minutes, I was subjected to a more intense version of Miss Morgan's swimming lessons, but instead of there being twenty of us, there were only five or six, including me. My teacher was an older girl. I was not very good at guessing the ages of older kids, but she was probably about fifteen, or maybe twenty-five. Much younger than Miss Morgan at any rate. She told me her name was Clair, but that people called her Mother Duck. An odd name, but it established credibility, from a swimming point of view.

Mother Duck set the others off on a four-width swim and asked me to wait as I held onto the rail. With the others gone she said, 'OK, Thomas, I want you to swim to the other side, as well as you can, and without stopping, all right?' I suddenly noticed that we were now a bit deeper than I was used to, and that there was a good chance my feet wouldn't be able to touch the floor when I got tired. I tried to touch the bottom, just to check, and only my toes made contact. I looked up at her anxiously. 'It's OK, Thomas, don't worry,' she said, reading my face, 'I'll be watching you all the way.' I didn't reply, but turned to face the other side of the pool. My massive goggles were already leaking water so I couldn't really see where I was heading. I set off in the most energetic way I knew how, hopeful that Mother Duck was as good as her word.

I kicked and kicked as hard as I could, and whirled my arms round and round as fast as possible. Just like at school it was exhausting, but I knew I had to keep going given I couldn't *quite* stand up. Eventually, I reached the other side, bumping quite hard into the wall I hadn't seen thanks to the leaky goggles. I pulled them down around my neck and immediately looked back to the other side, hoping to see a look of approval for my efforts. I'd surprised myself by getting across without stopping and was tired, but pleased. She wasn't there, where I'd left her. I frowned – all that effort and no recognition.

'Well done, young Thomas.' I turned around and looked up. Mother Duck was standing above me on the same side of the pool, smiling to herself. Standing next to her was a short, stocky man with a largely bald head, a sharp nose and a stern expression. He was built like a cannonball. He wore smart grey flannel trousers and a white t-shirt, on top of which was an even smarter blue cardigan, with two white hoops on each sleeve. His gleaming white tennis shoes stood out against the grey trousers. He was about Dad's age, maybe a bit older, but there any similarity ended. He didn't have a beard for a start. And he looked to be very much in charge.

'Who's this?' he said to Mother Duck while looking at me.

'This is young Thomas. It's his first night.' In that moment I began to understand why she had the name she did.

The cannonball nodded at me without smiling, his eyes fixed on mine. 'Do what Mother Duck tells you,' he said firmly. I nodded back in silence from the water. 'You'll need to get an orange club swimming hat . . . and some proper goggles.'

With that, John Bullet walked off, and my summer of swimming began.

*

In the end, that summer turned out to be as good as any summer could be. The new house had become something of an adventure after all. Nearby there were large parks, perfect for flying kites, and even tennis courts. Anna, who suddenly seemed to know a lot about tennis, had her own smart new wooden tennis racket – a 'McEnroe Junior', which was too heavy for me. We played on the immaculate public grass courts, which were often empty despite being so well kept by a nice man who worked for the council. There were also woods to be found with some exploration, and some big slopes that would be useful if it ever snowed.

Since that first session at the baths, Mum had made us go to the swimming club every Wednesday night and I was slowly changing my opinion of it. I was still being taught in the same group of kids, but only sometimes got to be taught by Mother Duck. There were other teachers of a similar age, all with odd nicknames. 'Miss Piggy' was my favourite of the other teachers, whose number also included 'Panda', 'Bear' and 'Shovel'.

My swimming was getting better. I could now swim two widths of the small pool after a rest halfway, and, thanks to my smart new Eyeline goggles, I could see where I was going. I'd started to learn a new stroke – breaststroke, which was harder and slower than front crawl. It required more coordination in order to avoid sinking, and if one of my feet made a splash when I kicked I was told off for having a 'screw kick' – both legs had to mirror each other. I was less keen about the bright orange swimming cap we all had to wear, as by the time it had sat in my bag for a week it was very firmly stuck together and hard to put on. Plus I thought I looked like an orange Smurf. Still, my progress at swimming more than made up for the silly hat.

Our choice of music had also improved dramatically now the cousins were on the scene. Anna had access to a seemingly limitless supply of cassettes, which, thanks to Vicky's special double tape-deck, could be re-recorded by Anna at will. Car journeys as a family had become more of a sing-along, provided there was no Test Match commentary which triggered Dad to veto all music. Anna, who was suddenly much more knowledgeable about nearly everything, had achieved a new level of brotherly respect anyway. She was able to explain why things, from girls, to the latest craze, or even Mum and Dad, were as they were, and in a way I could understand.

As September and its new term arrived, school seemed far less intimidating than the year before. The new term brought with it new people, as our class grew bigger with the addition of a couple more boys. One of them, Roger Ratajczak, sat next to me. I liked Roger from the moment I met him. As he introduced himself – he was very polite – I knew he was unlike anyone else in our class. I told him he had an unusual name, and he agreed. He said it was harder to spell than it was to say (it rhymed with 'Crackerjack', like the TV show). I was glad to be a Gregory once he wrote it down for me. In the weeks that followed we became best friends. Roger (sometimes known as Rat-Bag) was a very confident companion, despite being so new, and much more knowledgeable about many things: girls, music and how to have fun. I, on the other hand, knew how things were at his new school, and so we made a good team. We even practised our French together in between lessons (we now had French lessons once a week) – essential given my desire to return to Brittany after a recent family holiday there.

Apart from having a scary new class teacher, Mr Fuller, things carried on very much as they had done, save for swimming lessons with Miss Morgan. I had already told Roger the main rules – do as Miss Morgan says, and don't talk at the same time as her unless you want to freeze to death; the school pool was outdoors, and so punishment for any collective misbehaviour was simply to stand in the open, dripping wet, until order had been restored. Fine in the summer, traumatic in the winter. In our first lesson of the term she set us off across the width in the very shallow end. To my astonishment, I was the fastest to the other side. Miss Morgan was still standing on the side of the pool where we left her, and so, buoyed by my triumph, I swam back, but quicker this time, leaving my classmates hanging on the rail.

'Well done, Thomas,' she said, beaming a magic smile. 'Have you had a busy summer?'

'Yes, Miss. Very busy,' I replied, adjusting my Eyeline goggles.

She summoned the class back to our side of the pool. As I watched my friends splash towards us, I realized that something important had happened. For the very first time, I was the best in the class at something, and *that something* happened not to be maths, or comprehension, or French, but . . . well . . . swimming. Good enough, I thought. And then I thought of Mother Duck and how I owed my progress to her and the other club swimmers.

September passed quickly with all the excitement of a new term, and, despite my best efforts, I failed to possess either a champion conker or an even near-complete football sticker album. In class I was struggling a little, too. Roger was good at keeping his concentration – despite my attempts to distract him – but I really was not. Mr Fuller had put a sign up on my desk that read 'Think Before You Ink'. I was the only boy who needed this reminder. By the time of my eighth birthday on 9 October, I was near the bottom of the all-important class 'plus' board, having only achieved a couple of hallowed 'plus' marks in homework assignments. 'Tommo' Thompson had twenty to his name already.

Even at the swimming club things had started to get harder. With the summer over, we were all required to return to the big pool and join the Senior swimmers, who, now the season was over, were resuming their training in warm water. The stories of the cousins had not been quite so fanciful after all; they had spent the summer swimming only in cold water, training in a place called the Lake District, and, according to Anna, had spent most of August and September on something called 'Channel Alert' – a dramatic term used by their dad, Uncle John, to describe the possibility of being sent to swim to France with their friends at very short notice. When they weren't doing all that, they were teaching younger kids, like me, to swim on a Wednesday night.

The big pool at Eltham was another proposition entirely. Not only was it very large, and very deep at one end, but it also had a daunting array of diving boards, the highest of which was the tallest I had ever seen. The ladder even had a safety rope to prevent accidental access, from which was suspended a cartoon sign warning of the danger of falling. In fact, there were lots of cartoons around the pool advising swimmers what to avoid. There was one caption that read 'No heavy petting!' and featured a couple, surrounded by hearts, which rose like balloons, kissing in the water. Clearly this was a regular occurrence at Eltham. As I considered the possibilities, I concluded the likelihood of my breaking that rule to be slim. My favourite poster was a kind of compendium, or 'best-of' all the rules not to be broken. It included prohibition on 'bombing, loud singing, splashing others, smoking' (presumably difficult while swimming) and 'running'. The big pool at Eltham was for Big People.

Wednesday night swimming now started half an hour later at 6.30. The changing rooms for the big pool were like caves that ran deep on either side of the sunken depth of the pool itself. Along the narrow and dark underground corridors ran huge water pipes, which hummed as they carried the vast amounts of water into and out of the old pool. I imagined that it felt like being in a submarine. Leaving the changing rooms I would climb the stairs to emerge on the poolside and squint in the bright lights, which contrasted so much with the dark cave below. The big pool was flanked by tall banks of tiered spectator benches on either side. The whole poolside and surrounding walls were tiled in a light brown colour, and on peering into the blue water, I could see that the surface of the pool itself consisted of thousands and thousands of small rectangular white tiles. The high roof seemed to cover an impossibly large area. It was an intimidating and noisy place.

Groups of parents would congregate in one corner of the spectator seating nearest the diving boards and watch the night unfold. I had begun to recognize some of their faces now. Some had jobs to do, like sell orange swimming hats, or collect 'subs' from members. Mr Overy, the chairman, would drum up support for social events and fundraising activities. Anna had explained that some families, like the Kents, Wetherlies and Waglands, were long-time supporters and members, with successive siblings having made their mark within the ranks of the club – now celebrating its eighteenth year. All of this activity took place under the direction of one man – John Bullet. Founder, coach, controller of all things.

The swimmers were split into three groups: Juniors, Intermediates and Seniors. To prevent chaos and collisions, the pool was segregated into three long zones by lane ropes that ran the entire length of the pool. The zones were wide – two or three lanes each, leaving room for the groups to swim up one side, and down the other.

As we assembled in our groups on the large poolside of the shallow end, I looked across at the Seniors, now together for the first time after the summer, and recognized some of my teachers from the previous few months. I could see the cousins, Carolyn and Victoria, along with Mother Duck, Miss Piggy and Bear. All were wearing a serious and focused expression underneath their orange rubber hats. There too was John Bullet, in his grey flannel trousers, smart woollen cardigan and clean white shoes. He appeared on the poolside next to the Senior group and barked a series of instructions. On this occasion he wore a shiny metal whistle on a lanyard around his neck.

'Right, shut up, you lot!' he began loudly, boring his eyes into those who dared speak. 'Twenty lengths crawl warm up, then straight into a 4x2 . . . Take your marks.' The swimmers jostled. 'Hurry UP!' he added impatiently. The swimmers shuffled into a line as John barked 'Go! . . . Go! . . . Go!' at each swimmer in turn, setting them off at short intervals. I looked on as they dived athletically and rhythmically into the pool, one by one like on a conveyor belt, and sped away down the length. I was instantly in awe of their ability to swim so far, and so fast.

As the noise levels in the baths rose, my own Junior group were put to work under the instructions of a woman called Tanya. I had never swum a length of the big pool before, and it looked easily to be further than two widths of the small pool – with nowhere to rest halfway. I resolved to stay close to the lane rope or the gutter channel of the pool, in case I needed to stop and hold on. I longed for Anna by my side, but she had already been moved into the Intermediate group.

'OK, you lot, let's have a look at you,' said Tanya. Six or seven of us, mostly kids I recognized from the small pool but with a couple of new faces, put our goggles on over the top of our orange hats. 'Let's have two lengths of your best front crawl, please . . .'

Two lengths?! I thought in a panic. I was unlikely to be able to complete one, let alone a second. I moved myself to the back of the queue to buy some time. Tanya knew most of our names already, but, as I got to the front of the queue, she asked who I was.

'My name is Thomas,' I replied.

'Ah, that's right – I was expecting you. OK, Thomas, off you go,' she said. I wondered why I had been *expected* at all. Perhaps she knew of Anna and me from the cousins.

I dived into the pool belly first and set off. My body instantly shivered. The big pool was much colder than the small pool and the sudden immersion underlined the extent of the transition between the two. After a few strokes my goggles leaked, probably as a result of the dive, so I paused to straighten them out, staying afloat, using the new breaststroke with just one arm, and keeping my head up as I did so. Underway again I watched as the pool below me deepened, and then deepened suddenly again as a steep ramp ran it down to maximum depth. I had never swum in water this deep, not knowingly at least, and with the far end of the pool still some way off there was only one thing to do – keep swimming.

To my surprise I was at the far end of the long pool soon afterwards and felt an acute sense of pride as I hung onto the rail in the shadow of the enormous diving boards. Tanya, seeing me stop from 30 metres away, waved her arms frantically to beckon me back, which suggested I had done something wrong. Suddenly nervous again, I set off towards the shallow end, consoled by the fact that, if I became exhausted as I approached the shallow end I might at least be able to stand up. I got tired, and it became harder to swim, and my arms started to ache with the effort. My head was barely getting above the water, and I had a moment of panic as, breathing heavily, I gulped in a lung-full of pool water. Stopping to recover, I floated on my back, and caught my breath. Looking up . . . just a few metres to go. The other kids were already on the poolside looking on. After a final effort, I made it to the rail, exhausted, embarrassed, and breathing very hard.

'Out you get,' said Tanya. There was no praise to be had. There was no Mother Duck either, who was busy swimming laps with the other Seniors. Bewildered, I pulled myself sideways along the rail towards the steps in order to climb out. 'No steps, Thomas – *pull* yourself out, please,' instructed Tanya. I tried to jump up from the water, where I could now stand up, and to haul myself out. This proved to be nearly as hard as the swim itself, and I could hear some of the other kids sniggering as I floundered, bouncing up and down, half in, half out, trying in vain to get a grip on the smooth tiles and pull my body clear from the water. Eventually out, I went to the back of the re-formed queue of swimmers, feeling nervous. To compound my misery Tanya added, addressing the group, 'Thomas, we don't stop at the deep end. We touch the end of the pool, turn and swim back. OK?' I nodded silently, wondering how things had come to this. From the back of the queue, still breathing heavily with reddened face, I looked up at the length of the pool in fear of what would come next. For the briefest moment, it struck me that I had just swum further, and in deeper water, than I had ever swum before, and having obeyed all the cartoon instructions, I hadn't drowned.

But then again, as with a few other things in my life at that time, I was last, again.

Things at the pool carried on like that for a while. I dreaded Wednesday nights. The routine at home was rushed; Mum would pick me up from school at 4 o'clock, and once home, feed me a hot bacon and egg sandwich. This normally coincided with my attempts at homework, which got less than my full attention on account of my anxiety over what was to come. It was not unusual for Mr Fuller to circle large areas of my exercise book with his red biro the next day, a shorthand form of enquiry regarding the presence on the pages of crumbs, normally framed by circular butter stains, or the odd blob of ketchup. With rushed homework left incomplete, I would chase around the house looking for my swimming kit. When (frequently) I was unable to find it, Mum normally had the answer. The rush continued.

Hearing the 6 o'clock news theme tune strike up from the TV, which, with its urgent and pushy tempo, also sounded rushed, my tummy would turn in knots – the tune marked the approaching moment to leave for the baths. Often I pleaded with Mum that I didn't want to go, and even became upset to the point of tears. Although Anna was unlikely to tell me or show it, I sensed that my sister had similar reservations. Mum would always reply that 'it would be fine', and not to be a baby. I wondered if Anna needed similar persuasion, but in more grown-up language when I was not listening. Meanwhile, at the club itself, things were still getting harder.

After a few weeks listening to instructions, normally from Tanya or Mother Duck, I was moved into the Intermediate lane, where Anna was also to be found and where most students were eleven years old or more, not eight like me, and happily lapping up the lengths. I didn't see my promotion as in any way welcome, because it simply meant the swimming had become much more challenging, which in turn resulted in my still being last all the time. In an attempt to keep up, I had renewed my efforts to listen carefully to the Seniors in recent weeks, who, I had come to accept, were there to help us swim better, with their barked orders from the poolside.

I had learned to 'kick from the hip' when swimming front crawl, instead of from the knee, and although it made the very top of my legs ache, I found it required fewer kicks per arm stroke once I got used to it. My arms had also improved. It had been explained to me that in any given point during front crawl, the 'underwater arm' needed to travel downwards and through the water in a wide, preferably vertical circle, rather than be recovered with a bent elbow towards the waist (which resembled the underwater equivalent of taking a bow). Again, this was harder to do at first, but it took fewer arm strokes to complete a length once I got the hang of it. I had also come to possess an imaginary line that split me in two vertically, and which my leading hand was not to cross at the point in the stroke when I reached out in front of me – always 'as far as you can'. My hands, when out of the water, were to be facing outwards, in an inverted wave – which looked like an army salute, only horizontally rather than stood to attention.

At some point in the process I found some balance between what my arms and legs were doing, which meant that breathing became easier; I no longer had to take the odd exhausted breath looking forwards (instead of to the side). I could also swim in a straight line, provided I kept an eye on the blue lane markings on the bottom of the pool, and my new goggles didn't leak. I'd even learned a trick that prevented my goggles from misting up, which was to lick them on the inside first and then fill them with pool water for thirty seconds, before finally putting them on my head.

But none of this new knowledge was enough to stop me from coming last in every set of lengths in the Intermediate group. The warm up alone was now ten lengths and normally enough to finish me off. Once the mixed-stroke sets started (I had been forced to learn them all quickly) things were fine during the backstroke, breaststroke and crawl sections, but the butterfly, which always came first in the list, was still a total mystery to me. I would have to get that sorted out as a priority. Meanwhile, Anna had got the whole thing sorted, and she always looked so good in the pool. Anna always knew how to make things look easy.

Neither school nor swimming club looked likely to become easier any time soon. But relief was at hand; Christmas of 1984 was undoubtedly the best Christmas ever, and for one reason only: I now owned a Walkman. Technically speaking it was not a 'Walkman' – they were made by Sony, and mine was made by Saisho – but that didn't matter. It played tapes and it came with bright orange foam-covered headphones. Mine was yellow, about the size of a half bag of flour, and heavy enough to require a shoulder strap; in other words, the very latest thing. It had a sliding volume adjuster amid some other important buttons on one side, and a radio dial at one end that could receive AM *and* FM. Best of all, it had a three band graphic equalizer on the front, the sliders moving up and down in their grooves. Even Anna was a little envious as I tore through the wrapping paper, though her envy almost immediately disappeared when, aged ten and three-quarters, she unwrapped her first album, to add to her nascent singles collection. Madonna's *Like a Virgin* was all hers, and she wanted for little else, as a log on the fire popped with festive approval.

'Don't think you can help yourself to my mix tapes, Little Brother,' she warned as I continued ripping open paper. I'd no intention of obeying Anna's instruction at that point, but the need was instantly removed upon opening my other present: not just a tape from Our Price, but a *double* tape called *Now That's What I Call Music 3*. I looked at the back of the chunky plastic cassette box and was thrilled to see that the first song on the compilation album was 'The Reflex' by Duran Duran. ('Have that, Tommo . . .' I thought.) Scanning down the long list there were other songs by pop stars I knew of, like Nik Kershaw, Frankie Goes to Hollywood and Wham!. It even had my favourite song, 'When You're Young and in Love' by the Flying Pickets. OK, so it didn't have Band Aid's 'Feed the World', which was the current number one and which everyone was talking about, but Anna had bought that on 7" anyway, so it didn't matter. Mum, being Mum, asked if she had 'got the right thing'. I delayed the impulse to do what I wanted to do and open the thing properly, and instead offered a gabbled reply – 'Thanks, Mum. Thanks, Dad. It's perfect' – before hastily resuming my present opening.

Later we sat as a family around the Christmas fireplace, which was roaring with a combination of logs and hot coals. As Mum and Dad looked on I hurriedly fumbled the batteries into the compartment and loaded the tape: cassette 1, side 1. I pushed the heavy plastic yellow play button on the side of the unit and the mechanism whirred magically into life. The spindles were visible through the window on the front of the yellow box. I sat wide-eyed on the floor, holding the box in front of me, the big orange headphones smothering my ears. The background fuzz kicked in and added to the sense of anticipation, but was suddenly interrupted by a computerish rising arpeggio, which was obviously the start of the tape formally announcing itself to *me*, the listener. Then, after a short pause . . . '*Ta-na Na-na . . . Ta-na Na-na . . . The Reflex . . . The Reflex*', louder and clearer than anything I had ever heard. The bass, rhythm and keyboards kicked in, followed quickly by Simon Le Bon's voice, and my head was suddenly full of the sound. It felt like the band were actually playing between my ears. I looked at Anna, at first open-mouthed and then laughing with joy. She smiled back at me, with a knowing look.

After a couple of months of heavy use, the only drawback I could see to my Walkman was the absence of a rewind button. It only had a fast forward button, marked FFD. I'd worked out that if I wanted to listen to the same song again, I had to flip the tape, fast forward the other side and guess when to stop, before flipping it back again. Apart from being annoying, the process was also an inexact science. Meanwhile, all the other aspects of my life seemed to be going the same way. Everything was on fast forward, and was also quite often annoying, and as with the tape, I was unable to rewind any of it.

School was getting harder by the week, and I continued to struggle to keep up. Not even Roger, who was now a major character in our class, could help me. The maths teacher, Miss Rowling, had asked Mum and Dad to come to school especially to discuss my progress, and particularly my homework. In the meeting, Mum reacted calmly when Miss Rowling asked if anything was 'amiss at home', but was later quite angry at the question. Feeling rather guilty, I resolved to try harder with maths. The long dark nights did nothing to cheer the mood hanging over January and February.

At a swimming club night around this time, something else new happened. John Bullet, who had never really spoken to me or Anna personally, or even had any cause to, decided that we were both to join the older kids for extra training on a Sunday morning. After our Wednesday night training session, Anna and I were summoned to John's office at Eltham Baths, where, as the cousins had repeatedly told me, he was also the general manager. I'd never been to John Bullet's office and we were both nervous. John was visibly in control of all things at the baths and within the club. He had a personal presence that commanded people's respect, and it was already clear to me that he was treated with a degree of deference by swimmers and parents alike. According to the cousins, he also had a reputation for having a short temper, and could sometimes be volatile. Since joining the club I had been torn between wanting him to notice me, in thrall to the respect he was held in, and keeping a low profile lest I make things any harder on myself.

We tentatively ventured through the large wooden door, on which was fixed a sign declaring him to be the 'Baths Manager'. We found John seated behind a big old wooden desk in the middle of the room. He was facing away from us and looking around the walls as if trying to locate something. The office was about the same size as Dad's, but instead of being surrounded by hundreds of dusty old legal books that all looked the same, John was surrounded by all things related to swimming, and to the running of a large public pool. There were trophies lined up on shelves, photographs of staff in bright orange t-shirts arranged on a board (lifeguards, I assumed), a wall planner of events, and reams of paperwork that sat on one side of his desk – smothered by a heavy glass paperweight. I noticed that the small windows were high up and had strong steel bars on the inside, which, along with the magnolia walls, gave the place the look of a prison cell. We waited for him to turn and speak to us. From up close I noticed the very clear dent in the back of his head, which ran from the top of his skull down towards his neck. It looked severe – as if caused by some great accident or adventure. To my shame, I couldn't help thinking that, were he a teacher at school, this would almost certainly have caused him to be nicknamed 'Mr Bum Head', but I kept this thought to myself.

'Anna, Thomas – you are to come to extra training on Sunday mornings from now on. Meet time is 9.30. You will be free by 11.30. Any questions?'

'No, John,' said Anna. I shook my head to indicate the same thing.

'Make sure you tell your parents,' he added.

'OK, John,' replied Anna.

'That's all.'

We walked out of the office. Dad was waiting in the pool foyer, having just finished a pint with Uncle John and some of the other parents from the club in the White Harte pub opposite the baths. 'Dad, we've been told to report for extra training on Sunday,' I said excitedly as I ran up to him.

'I know, son. I know.'

I wondered *how* he knew, and assumed that Uncle John must have had some inside information.

As we left the baths that night I glanced across at the club display board that was bolted to the wall in the large entrance hall of the baths, and which was protected by a locked glass screen. Across the top read 'Eltham Training and Swimming Club'. I noticed the mass of black and white photographs and press cuttings of swimmers, both past and present, who had presumably done great things. It was a Hall of Fame. The older, yellowed cuttings showed kids wearing flares and tank tops that dated them as from a decade ago or more. In some photos they appeared in groups of six, in others they were on their own. The groups were all smiling, and either holding up certificates or huddled together in heavy clothing in wild-looking surroundings. The lone swimmers were normally pictured in action, with hat and goggles on, either entering or coming out of the sea. They also seemed to be covered in a white lotion – probably sun cream, I thought. I wondered if Carolyn and Victoria were in any of the photographs and whether Anna or I would ever do anything good enough to get on the notice board too. I wouldn't mind being famous, I thought, especially before Anna.

6.15 a.m., 6 September 1988 – 1 hour, 2.5 miles off the French coast, English Channel

I knew that the darkness that enveloped me would shortly be lifted as dawn began its daily conquest of the English Channel, delivering a new day, Tuesday 6 September 1988, into the Dover Strait. Daybreak would herald a maritime transition from one set of rules to another. I had never experienced this transitory phase from the sea, let alone swum through it. Come to that, I had never really experienced the darkness either, especially not offshore. We had done some night swimming in Dover harbour, but the black water near the shoreline had still been bathed in the yellow lights of the promenade, and our bright orange hats must have been as bright as stars in the night sky when set against the water and reflected light.

The dark hours this morning had been the most exciting hours of my life. The fishing boat rendezvous had worked smoothly. By the time I caught up with the trawler (I had to look forwards every few strokes and pick out her lights to avoid getting lost), the tender was tied on, the occupants had boarded the larger vessel and it all looked to be calm and organized. Up close the boat was larger than I had expected; it was carrying more people than I had expected too. The wheelhouse was near the bow and had a hard covering on three sides, with a sliding door facing the stern. Forward of the wheelhouse 'FE41' was stencilled in large white letters across what looked in the dark like navy-blue painted bows. The registration marking was visible even in the darkness. There was a small amount of deck space forward and the prow of the boat looked stubby and industrial. The gunwales that led up to the bow rose steeply, protecting the main boat and giving the impression she was built for heavy weather. Behind the wheelhouse was the large flat working area. I wondered how many fish Willy could catch when he wasn't escorting people like me. A heavy but open-sided canvas canopy was held in place by a metal frame, and a pair of neon strip lights were stationed on the underside to illuminate the area completely. It was a harsh light – sterile and cold, not cosy or warm. Good, less reason to want to join the passenger list. Watching the activities of the occupants was like peering into a large floating dolls' house. Along with the motion of the sea, it was vaguely hypnotic. I had come to love the sensations of sea swimming – the movement of the water and of my body's smooth path through it. It was roughly three and a half years since I had first experienced this, over Easter.

In 1985, there was no family roast at Easter. Instead Anna and I reported to the baths early on the Saturday morning for extra training. Not at the pool this time. The Easter long weekend was to be spent camping with the older kids, *teenagers*, 70 miles down the A2 near Dover, for *cold water* training. The fast forward button had been pressed again . . . And this time it was stuck.

There was limited information available on what was likely to take place at Dover, save for the inevitability of getting wet and cold. The cousins just said that there would be a lot of swimming, but added casually that we ought not to worry about it. I *was* worried about it. And so was Anna. On the Wednesday night before the camp itself we were each handed a typed letter on official-looking swimming club letterhead, which advised us what to pack. Once home I handed my copy directly to Mum for the maternal oversight I craved, even though it guaranteed a level of interference in the days to come. There were some more hints about what to expect in the packing list:

Woolly hat and gloves
Thick jumpers
Thermal underwear, and spares
Waterproof jacket
Slacks *(what were slacks?)*
Swimming kit and towel, to include spare hat and goggles
Sleeping bag – no pillow
Wash kit

Report times (7.30 a.m. on the Saturday) and expected return times (mid-afternoon, Easter Monday) were in there, as was a requirement to pay £5 to the club secretary. Other than that there was little to go on.

The night before we left the house, Mum, who was notably anxious about the whole thing, 'prepared' the most enormous meal of Marks and Spencer's Chinese Chicken – boxes of the stuff. Anna and I had discovered a love of this expensive form of fast food after Mum had bought some by accident and nearly incinerated the contents in our new-fangled microwave. As we gorged our way through the pile of sticky, spicy red chicken, Mum offered me some advice. 'Tom-Tom. Remember to put your shoes at the end of your sleeping bag when you go to bed.

It may be that John Bullet is a military man, and people like that appreciate such things.' Baffled, I returned to the pile of chicken. Anna, who was unusually silent, devoured as much as she could, fearing the catering arrangements that lay ahead.

The next day we arrived, packed, nervous, but on time, only to find others had been there even earlier. The Seniors had been busy loading a minibus and its rickety roof rack with a large amount of communal camping equipment that had emerged from a lock-up within the precincts of the baths. The minibus itself was old. The white Bedford, with its rounded lines and bulbous curves, looked very much to be from the 1960s. It reminded me of the old police vans from various dated TV shows that were on after I was supposed to have gone to bed. It even had an old-style number plate, just like the cars in the London to Brighton vintage rally. There was rust all over it, like spots on a Dalmatian dog, and, on both sides, in broken and fading letters, the words 'Eltham Training and Swimming Club' were stencilled in what was once a dark blue.

The bus, now packed and loaded under the supervision of Mother Duck, was already straining on its axles under the weight, but was ready for its passengers. John Bullet appeared, dressed in his normal attire of cardigan and t-shirt, but with a sportier-looking pair of trousers. Perhaps these were *slacks*.

'Right, let's go. I fuckin' 'ate traffic,' John announced with a stern expression, climbing urgently into the driving seat as he did so. I glanced around quickly, hoping Dad had left. He would have raised an eyebrow at the swearing, even though Anna and I knew all the worst words. But Dad was long gone, and then I suddenly wished him back.

The group of us, about fourteen, clambered in. There were only ten seats in the back, but the spare tyre that sat between the rearmost benches and just in front of the bulbous back doors formed an extra one. As the smallest by some margin, I was told to squash in among the bags in the aisle between the double benches. I did as I was told, relieved not to have to sit next to any of the girls, secretly hopeful that I had been conferred the status of group mascot. I was by far the youngest, with Anna, three years my elder, the youngest after that. I felt out of place; to me the other swimmers were closer to adulthood than childhood.

The engine spluttered into life, and the gears ground heavily until one was located. As we rolled out onto Eltham High Street, the noise levels inside the bus steadily increased as multiple conversations began. Loud pop music suddenly added to the din. It was Wham! and was coming from a big silver stereo on Miss Piggy's lap. The girls alternated between their excited conversations and singing along. The boys tried to mask their secret approval by rolling their eyes, and instead picked out the flashiest cars on the road. Justin Palfrey (one of the few swimmers not to have a nickname, and the fastest swimmer in the club) then unleashed a vicious fart from his position on the spare wheel seat. He grinned, smugly, amid howls of protest from his fellow passengers. There was some laughter, a firm punch to Palfrey's thigh from Bear, and a reprimand from John in the driver's seat as he struggled to wind down his window. The chaos continued.

I remained wedged among a pile of kit bags, nervous, excited and wide-eyed. This was my first trip away from home without my parents or grandparents, and I would probably have refused to go the night before, in a flood of eight-year-old tears, but for Anna. We had sat up late in her room, bags packed, anxiously discussing what might occur. She was nervous too, but she trusted in the cousins, and I, in turn, trusted in Anna. Meanwhile, Mum and Dad, it seemed, trusted in John Bullet.

Anna, who like me had said nothing for a while, sat still, quietly mouthing the words to whichever song was playing. The early morning Easter sunshine lifted spirits still further as we filtered onto the A2. I wondered what Mum, Dad and our dog Flossie were up to. Probably on their way to the special secret café on Shooters Hill . . .

From my nest of bags I became steadily more nervous as we neared the coast. Dover was getting closer, just 5 miles away according to the last signpost. My tummy turned in a knot . . . What would happen now? Would we just drive up to the seafront somewhere and be told to get in and swim? Would it be *very* cold? Would I freeze to death, or be unable to get in? What if I had forgotten something? As the bus pulled off the dual carriageway just outside Dover, I felt the sudden urge to cry.

After a few minutes winding our way down some country lanes we arrived at a large campsite where a sign read 'Martin Mill'. The bus had gone quiet after the initial euphoria on the A2. Now everyone looked a little reserved. John drove into a clearing – a small field partitioned from elsewhere by its own hedges and trees. No one spoke.

'Let's get on with it,' he announced, cutting the silence. The doors of the old bus burst open, and the Seniors sprang into action, just like in *The A-Team*. As swimmers scaled the sides of the Bedford and worked loose the ropes holding the luggage in place on the roof, bags tumbled off and began to form a pile on the grass. Teams of two or three waited below to catch the very heavy canvas bags of tentage and poles, while large crates of tinned food and other gear appeared from elsewhere. This was clearly a well-practised drill, but not one that Anna or I knew.

Within an hour the field had become our shared home. There were three large tents arranged in an open square: the boys' tent, the girls' tent and the food tent. The tents were unlike others I had seen – very large, made of a single layer of heavy canvas, and box shaped. They were held up by frames of strong metal poles that seemed quite complex to construct, yet no one referred to, or needed, any instructions. Guy lines were run out from every corner and fastened to large wooden stakes, rammed home with heavy mallets. Inner tents were erected to sleep in, thick canvas matting from a boxing ring laid for a floor in the sleeping quarters, and, in the food tent, a camping kitchen assembled and rations stowed. Water canisters, not to be moved, were placed outside each tent in case of fire. With bewildering pace things had come together.

In the boys' tent sleeping bags were rolled out, like multicoloured keys on a piano. There was clearly a hierarchy. My sleeping bag had been laid out for me at one end. John Bullet's was at the other. In between, I gradually deduced, the bags were roughly in order of age and so ability to swim in cold water. I had been particularly scared about the sleeping arrangements; partly because nothing was discussed in advance, and partly because there was a lack of information regarding life in the boys' tent – Anna and the cousins simply saw it as a mystery. Nonetheless, my bed was made, and our camp soon looked as though it had been there for weeks.

Then it started to rain.

'OK, on the bus then,' ordered John.

I collected my swim bag from the pile and followed others into the bus, relieved to get out of the rain, which had grown heavier. Leaving the campsite behind, we motored off back through the country lanes, the minibus clipping the hedges as we bowled along. The tunes on the stereo resumed, but there was no talking this time. The music was filling what would otherwise have been a tense silence. As we turned off the country lanes and onto a main road marked Jubilee Way, I glimpsed the sea for the first time through a huge road cutting. The dual carriageway swept its way down through the chalk cliffs above Dover. It was so steep and fast there were even escape-lanes for runaway trucks to crash into on one side, with big piles of sand and shingle to stop them. There were towering and important-looking radio masts on the tops of the cliffs – probably to detect hostile Russian aircraft, I thought.

We descended noisily, John using the gearbox to control the speed of the bus, and as we progressed through the cutting in the cliff towards Dover harbour, my heart began to thump with excitement at the magnificent scene that unfolded below us under the wet, grey rolling sky.

Massive ferries, bound for France and who knew where else, lay in dock, connected to giant gantries that loaded them with queuing cars. The circular length of the harbour wall stretched out to sea like enormous concrete arms, as if trying to gather the water back in towards the white cliffs. As we descended the tarmac slide I saw for the first time the promenade of Dover on the right through the drizzle. The grand-looking buildings along the seafront reminded me of Brighton. Beyond the promenade, the long harbour beach was spread out, bounded by the concrete walls on either side. The beach looked pebbly from a distance – like Brighton, not sandy like France.

I looked out at the brown, turning sea, stretching to the horizon. Its surface looked very different either side of the harbour wall. Beyond the harbour the sea was alive and crested with white specks. Ferries travelled to and fro. Inside the harbour the water looked calmer, but rippled and busy nonetheless. I perched on some kit bags to get a better view, only to find that the bus had travelled so quickly down the giant ramp that we were nearly at the bottom, and turning sharply round a right-hand bend. It was over too quickly. This was the most exciting road in the world by far. A giant helter-skelter, which felt perilous to travel, let alone drive down. I was suddenly glad John Bullet was at the wheel – he looked like someone who could be trusted to handle it.

John parked the bus on the seafront, which, despite the Bank Holiday weekend, was nearly empty, no doubt on account of the rain. The music stopped abruptly, and still no one spoke. John cut through the silence once more from the driver's seat. 'Right, you lot. Get changed.'

Another rush of nerves, another knot in my stomach. The doors to the bus slid open again, but slowly this time, as the swimmers, kit bags in hand, made for the protection of one of the shelters on the promenade, which were dotted along the front at regular intervals. They looked like posh bus stops: made of painted white iron and wood, with ornate details all over, and with long benches to sit on either side. I followed some of the others to the bench facing the sea. The boys had ended up on one side and the girls on the other. The swimmers began to get changed out in the open and I realized there was a skill to be mastered in using a towel to avoid a naked moment when putting trunks on in public. Still no one said anything.

One by one the swimmers put on the rubber orange swimming hats, whose real purpose immediately became clear as their brightness stood out against the wet early-April sky and dark backdrop of the sea. A man strolled by under an umbrella, his face a mixture of confusion and surprise. We looked odd – fourteen children with bright orange rubber heads, in swimming costumes, standing outside in a shelter avoiding the rain.

'Right, now. I want you IN, UNDER – and I mean UNDER – then OUT!' barked John loudly. 'No fannying around. Just get in, and get it done.'

I joined the procession down to the water's edge, across the pebbles and through the rain. The tide was in, so there wasn't far to walk, but the stones hurt my feet. I heard a desperate-sounding noise, looked up from the stones and saw that Mother Duck was already in the sea. She had cried out involuntarily at the moment she became fully immersed. Rather than get straight out as instructed, she stayed afloat, treading water in the freezing sea. She called out to the group, who hesitated on the edge of the water. I shivered in the rain, at the back. 'Come on, guys, it's not that bad,' she encouraged, struggling for breath, and with a smile that seemed to mask some amount of pain.

One by one the swimmers walked into the brown sea – ducklings forced to comply, lest they risk abandonment. The beach came alive with a fusion of screaming, shrieks and angry shouts. I could delay the moment no longer and pulling the goggles onto my eyes walked in up to my ankles. The shock of the cold made my feet hurt. Fearful of being last I took a big step forwards only to find the stones had vanished beneath me and so I tipped forwards into the deep water. My body convulsed and my lungs filled up in one huge involuntary gasp. Pain gripped my body and there was a moment of panic. Was this sudden death? My head moved rapidly from side to side trying to process the moment, my arms and legs keeping me afloat with their unplanned movements. Gasping, I looked over, tears in my eyes, and saw Mother Duck, floating, calmly now, and still treading water. 'Under you go, Young Marcus,' she said.

'Young Marcus' was my new nickname, conferred on me by John himself. I hadn't liked it initially. I preferred Tom to Thomas, but Thomas was certainly better than Marcus. But Anna had been kind about it. She explained that Marcus was a reference to Marcus Hooper, the greatest swimmer in the club's history, and current world record holder for age. He had been just twelve when in 1979 he swam from England to France in fourteen hours and thirty-seven minutes, becoming the 232nd person ever to have done so. Now grown up, he was no longer a member, but his photo was the most famous of those on the board in the foyer of the baths in Eltham. Not such a bad thing, then.

Without thinking I sank down and let the brownish grey water cover my head by some inches. I expected to touch stones, but my feet found none. At high tide the pebble beach sloped steeply. The underwater murkiness scared me, so I kicked up to the surface. Above water, but seeing only black now, I instinctively swam for the shore. I clambered onto the pebbles and stood up, gasping. Then the pain vanished. It was replaced by something far better, like being supercharged with electricity, and I no longer felt cold. I danced quickly up the beach, arms out wide to balance me across the painful stones. Climbing the sea wall to get to the shelter, I noticed John standing quietly, surveying the scene with a blank expression, arms folded. He hadn't moved. He glanced over casually. 'Well done, Young Marcus.' He looked back out towards his swimmers. 'Now get yourself dry and changed quickly. D'you hear?'

'Yes, John,' I replied, and although I didn't feel cold, my body was shaking. Others had made it back to the shelter already and were in a similar condition, struggling to dress themselves with shaking hands. I looked back to the water. Mother Duck and Miss Piggy were still in there, bobbing around happily. John waved them in from the shelter and I wondered how many more times we would go through this torture before going home.

The bus made its way back up Jubilee Way as fast as it could, which was not very fast at all; maximum revs in a low gear – heating on full blast. My body felt strange. My skin was still tingling, and even though I wasn't cold, I was still shaking. My clothes felt more comfortable and cosy than usual. The rain had finally stopped and, excited about driving up the helter-skelter road again, I perched myself up on the pile of bags. But instead of peeking out the window, I found myself staring at Miss Piggy, again. In fact, I had been looking at her more than anything, or anyone, else since we left London. This time she caught me, and looked back with a puzzled expression. I had been discovered. My face reddened.

She smiled at me, and held a perfect expression, tilting her head to one side a little and studying my reaction. A tidal wave of something, entirely new, washed over me as we looked at each other. Like the electric shock of the cold water, though it came from inside, it felt warm when the rest of my body was cold. She laughed a little, still looking at me, her blonde hair framing her fresh face. She had kind eyes. She was beautiful. The warm-inside sensation continued; like excitement, but with something extra added to the mix. The song playing on her stereo provided the live soundtrack to this moment of discovery – a slow number by Phil Collins – the added effect of the music almost more than I could stand. A lump appeared in my throat and my stomach turned in yet another knot. I had forgotten all about Jubilee Way, the cold, and swimming for that matter. This must be what it was like to be in love. Perhaps camping in Dover had more to offer than a Sunday roast after all.

Miss Piggy's real name was Alison. She was probably fifteen – roughly double my age – and had swum the Channel on her own, aged twelve like Marcus, just a couple of years ago in 1983. It had taken her sixteen hours and four minutes. As the only successful Channel soloist in the current group, she held the status of being the best swimmer. Many of the photos and press clippings on the notice board I had been studying were of her. Her crossing was, for a matter of hours, the girls' world record for age until it was broken by a rival swimmer, Samantha Druce, who was forty-three days younger. In the final mile Miss Piggy had swum through Dover harbour itself, stopping all ferry traffic in the process. Miss Piggy was a real-life legend.

As the bus approached the campsite, John announced from behind the wheel that he had put the 'wrong petrol in the tank'. The faces, pre-emptive giggling and jeers of the others told me they knew what was coming. The 'Kangaroo petrol' caused the bus to lurch violently back and forth, as John alternated his foot between accelerator and brake pedals. I and my fellow swimmers, for whom the old bus had no seatbelts, were thrown around in fits of laughter and pain. Shortly afterwards someone asked John if the 'hedges needed another trim'. They did, of course, and so the bus veered chaotically again, this time from side to side down the country lane, ripping away foliage as it went to the merriment of all on board. John, who I'd never seen like this before, was laughing hysterically from the driving seat – a frenzied look in his eyes, just visible to me from snatched glimpses in the rear-view mirror.

As the weekend unfolded, and my nervousness subsided, I realized I was having fun. In fact, *everyone* was having fun, including John, who, although strict when it came to swimming, was more mischievous and boyish than his poolside demeanour until now had suggested. It was exciting to be here – with the older kids. And John, who created a sense of reverence and revelry around him, seemed to be the oldest kid of all.

2. *The North*

6.30 a.m., 6 September 1988 – 1¼ hours, 3 and a bit miles off the French coast, English Channel

The state of the sea just off the French coast was unlike anything I had experienced before. The swell created an aquatic roller-coaster, and I was loving every second. The depth of the peaks and troughs increased dramatically as I swam out due west from the shelter of Wissant Bay. If I judged my distance from the boat and my breathing well enough, I could momentarily look down onto the deck and its occupants from a peak, just as the vessel rolled herself into a trough. That's how I knew about the sea-sick passenger. FE41 was moving slowly, at the pace of a swimmer, so her engines were unable to steady her rolling by powering her through the sea. She was like a Weeble toy, wobbling and bobbing in the darkness. No wonder someone was feeling ill.

I, on the other hand, was part of the sea. As the water rose and fell rhythmically I found I knew instinctively what to do; to hold an arm of front crawl out for a fraction longer, pull a bit harder on recovering an arm, or delay a breath momentarily to avoid a gulp of water. The sensation of travelling downwards reminded me of roly-polys on the grass in our local park. But the sea was smooth at the same time. Unlike Dover harbour, there was barely any chop and so, presumably, hardly any wind, although I had no reference points to prove this in the dark. The sheer scale of things, from the boat to the wave heights and the as yet unrevealed black distance ahead of me, was enthralling. 'One chance,' I said out loud as I breathed out.

Underwater something magic was happening. If I got further away from the boat and its nasty neon strip lights, I saw that my arms were somehow making their own flashes of light underwater. There were minuscule sparkles of blue or green within the blackness when I plunged an arm in and looked forwards. I thought I was imagining it at first, but it kept happening – the harder I drove my arm on entry the more likely it was to be visible. Mesmerized, I focused on nothing else but making the water light up for a while. Having perfected the technique as best I could, I glanced over for the boat – she was suddenly a long way off and members of the crew were waving and calling me back from over the rail. I had become distracted. I laughed and swam back to the boat where the magic light was no longer visible. Behind us the sky was gradually changing colour. Black was becoming dark blue, and not long after, there were tinges of pink where the water met the sky. I wondered what weather was coming in.

The night shift, just over an hour of adrenaline-enhanced swimming, had been an adventure, and kind to me. Not since the sun rose on that misty dawn on the shore of Windermere's southern tip two years before had I felt such a sense of place, or of belonging in the moment. Windermere: of all the locations John took us to prepare for this place, that was the one that counted for most.

I was out of breath. The climb was getting steeper, and every time I thought we were getting to the top of 'the hill', another ridge appeared. I was starting to wonder how big the hill was, given that the top had not been visible from the campsite where we set off. We could be climbing a *mountain*, here in the Lake District. When I looked back down to the campsite I could still make out our three familiar tents, now erect, but still flapping in the strong wind that blew down through the fell. They nestled neatly alongside the tree-lined stream that ran through a lush and steep-sided valley. Everything in the Lake District was a shade of green. The white minibuses stood out in contrast, each now the size of a Lego piece viewed from on high. The older people were doing various jobs setting things up. They looked like the miniature plastic figures in a game of soldiers. John, who seemed to be in a temper after the all-night drive, had told 'us lot' to 'Go and climb the hill!' clearly wishing us out the way. Bear (hairy body), who had been to Windermere before, said this was normal. So a few of us set off across the campsite, found a footpath that pointed uphill and started climbing. The mountainous valley near Lake Windermere was the most dramatic place I had ever seen – even better than the road into Dover. But if I stopped to think for too long, about *anything*, I knew I would start crying again. So I kept climbing.

Just getting here had been another adventure. Since Dover that Easter of 1985, the fast forward feeling had been replaced by a new sense of excitement, even confidence. Anna and I were now somehow and suddenly part of the Senior squad, and, having been on two more camps to Dover, had broadly got the hang of things. Swimming in the sea so early in the year was very cold. The time spent in the water had increased steadily over the trips to five, ten and then twenty minutes, and it was normal for some kids to leave the sea in a state of deep cold: shaking, with blue lips, even unable to dress themselves without help. I noticed that the kids who suffered most tended to be the skinny ones. Anna and I got cold, but were able to cope, being neither fat nor thin. As summer set in and the sea began its slow, stubborn warming up process, the Dover trips were supplemented by midweek evening swims in the local open air lido, sometimes in darkness, instead of the warm comfort of Eltham Baths. The physical challenge changed; from one of coping with the shock of cold, to one of resilience.

It was hard to know to what extent the sea had become warmer versus our bodies becoming acclimatized to the immersion. Anna thought it had to be a combination of those things.

I had learned a lot about swimming in the open conditions of the sea. Getting changed outside and in public was the easy part. Swimming in the rain – clearly not an issue. But wind and tide were things to think about. Even in the confines of Dover harbour the conditions could get choppy, but at beaches like St Margaret's-at-Cliffe on the north side of the harbour, or Shakespeare Cliff to the south, the waves could make normal swimming impossible, especially if a storm had passed through. Swimming in harsh conditions sometimes became a matter of staying afloat and judging how to time and handle the waves. When a wave caught the hand or arm when recovering mid-stroke, my breathing and balance were thrown, which normally meant coughing on a mouthful of saline, which could in turn make me retch and stop swimming entirely. When I asked John about it, he told me to straighten my arms a little at the elbow to keep them 'higher' – the action reminded me almost of a cricket bowl when he mimed it on the shore. My higher arm was less likely to hit the wave on its way through. It worked. Feelings of fear were being replaced by confidence, in my own abilities and the people around me. I liked it. It felt far better than being at school, where I was still frequently pulled up for bad habits or sloppy work.

When going along the shoreline in better weather, it was even possible to go backwards while swimming forwards if the tide was running quickly. Sometimes people were stung by jellyfish. The red rashes that resulted looked very unpleasant but conferred a level of status. However, I liked this type of swimming. There was nothing I could do to change the tide, or waves or wind, so every swim felt like a duel with the elements and a matter of survival. I knew, with John watching from the shore and the other swimmers around me, that I would be OK.

No one could enjoy the really cold feeling after a swim, which normally happened when the conditions meant I didn't notice I was cold until it was too late. I didn't like the saltiness of the water either. It tasted horrible, made my tongue sore, and could make me throw up. Saline also made things rub until they became sore, sometimes raw and bleeding: around the trunks, and especially armpits. Anna knew to carry some Vaseline, but often I forgot, only to ask Anna for a smear of grease to ease the soreness after it had happened.

Girls were still better at this kind of thing as far as I was concerned. Many of the boys in the group were faster, but not all of them could handle the cold. And the only person I knew who had actually *swum* the Channel was Miss Piggy. Just looking at her made me tremble. If she said anything to me, which was sadly a rare occurrence, I was excited beyond measure and could never manage much more than a blush in reply.

Even though we had learned quite a lot about swimming outside, neither Anna nor I had expected to be invited to Lake Windermere to train for a week once school broke up. Apart from anything else, we had agreed during a recent game of 'across-the-road badminton' that we were probably both a bit young for this, especially me. Anna was eleven, I was eight. The rest of the group, with one or two exceptions, were teenagers. But as a team, the two of us would cope. Anna would look out for me, and the older cousins would look out for Anna. John, meanwhile, would look out for everyone.

I had come to trust him – we both had – even though I was still scared of him. He was like a strict teacher from school – feared initially, becoming progressively more likable. I had begun to understand he was different from the other adults I knew, and certainly different from my parents – from Dad. A sense of mischief and nonconformism was ever present even though things had to be done in a certain way, from the trivial (the making of tea) to the critical (life-saving drills in the water). I was used to my parents' attitudes, which were, by and large, quite relaxed on most issues. The importance of these 'things', the things John cared about, was rarely appreciated by 'dozy parents' or 'idle teachers'. John's world, I was discovering, was forged in experience and practical application, rather than in text books. But humour, manifest in the obsession with nicknames (normally quite near the mark, and sometimes clearly beyond it), was an important facet. This was a tight-knit group, where banter and mickey-taking were constant, and, given the need for resilience, probably necessary. If someone was sensitive, it just got worse until they learned to cope with it or, if they couldn't cope with it, they usually left. Overall, though, Anna said that although she thought John had favourites, which were not always related to swimming prowess as much as to a sense of fun, things were basically 'fair' – an important concept in our family.

We arrived at the meeting point, the Yorkshire Grey pub car park at the foot of Eltham Hill, at 2 a.m. one Friday night in July. John 'fuckin' 'ated' traffic, so we would drive through the night. We were on time, but again others had done the hard work to get us ready to leave. The only thing the party needed was a full complement of nervous young swimmers from Eltham, whose parents had agreed to send them on an adventure to the Lake District.

I had never been out of bed so late and at 2 a.m. Eltham was asleep. Dad drove us down the deserted High Street without saying much at all. Anna had held my hand in the back seat. Mum, who always put a brave face on new things, had been very reassuring as we left home, but could tell I didn't want to leave and that I was fighting back tears. When Dad cuddled me to say goodbye in the car park I wanted to cry again, but I didn't want to look like a sissy, so I held it in.

The quiet of the night added to the tension. A silent tussle between the yellow streetlamps and the surrounding darkness offered a sense of danger. The brief moment where the night felt exciting was soon overpowered by a feeling of nauseous fear. On this occasion, I hoped I would be allowed to sit next to Anna on the bus.

There were two minibuses this time: the usual one full of the normal kit and support equipment required for swimming in a large lake, and a more road-worthy one hired for twelve or so swimmers. We would travel in convoy. John Bullet drove the rusty old club van and Dennis, Miss Piggy's dad, drove the hire bus with us, his passengers. 'Throw your bag into the kit bus, Young Thomas,' said Dennis kindly, referring to me by my real name, which was now used more often than 'Marcus'. I was happy that my real name had been returned to me, but sad to have lost the automatic association with the club's world record holder; I had learned a lot more about his swim in the preceding months just by reading the boards in the pool – trying to understand. I didn't have an all-important nickname yet. Everyone else did. It left me feeling a little sensitive, but not as sensitive as I might have felt on having an obvious bodily feature singled out.

Dennis fiddled in the near darkness with a wire coming from a very tall aerial that sat on the roof of his bus, like a limpet mine, thanks to a strong magnet on the base. Each bus was fitted with a Citizen Band, or 'CB', radio, so the drivers could communicate. I loved radios and walkie-talkies, and for a brief moment forgot all about my fear and watched in fascination, ignoring the instruction regarding my bag.

Next, Dennis fiddled with some red and black wires at the

back of the unit in the cab of the bus and suddenly the face of the CB buzzed into life and lit up the darkness. A bright red number shone out – 16 – the channel in use; next to this, a white back-lit meter with a vertical needle inside leapt into life when Dennis squeezed the microphone – the needle swinging quickly across into the red area of the dial. It looked very scientific. There was a volume switch and something called a 'Squelch' dial, which, when Dennis fiddled with it, caused the radio to issue an urgent and constant *chhhhhhhhchhh* sound. I had never seen anything like this and knew instantly that I loved CB radios.

'JB, JB, this is Dennis the Menace . . . OVER!' said Dennis into the black plastic mic. After a moment, John Bullet's voice came back through the same mic, all the way from the other side of the car park. *'Menace, Menace, this is JB, JB. Roger, loud and clear. Ten-four.'* Dennis twisted some dials, the set went quiet, and he turned to another task. I stood staring at the CB, still glowing in the darkness, mesmerized.

We drove through London's deserted streets in silence and I saw my city in a new way. All the traffic lights were green, and the hushed hours felt dangerous, even though there was no one to be seen. I recognized our route through the South London boroughs of Peckham and Southwark.

The city changed. As we crossed the Thames over Westminster Bridge the lights of Parliament reflected back at me from the black flowing river. Westminster looked serious and magnificent. The lights round Buckingham Palace were less bright and more spaced out. Their icy white shimmer somehow gave the place a sense of added importance. I looked for the flag to see if the Queen was in, but with none visible decided she must also be on holiday. Recognizing the exciting landmarks as we sped by (Marble Arch was next) meant I knew roughly where I was, which was a comfort and kept me occupied. But at some point soon afterwards, the landmarks, and all the things I recognized, ended. We filtered onto a motorway called the M1. The large blue road sign showed distances to places I had heard of, like Birmingham, and at the bottom the sign confirmed that this was the way to 'THE NORTH'. But the North was so far away it had no distance quoted, not yet. Miss Piggy's stereo was now playing quietly, and nearly all of the swimmers were asleep. As we rolled steadily up the motorway, further and further from home, and from Mum, Dad and Flossie, I kept looking out the window, even though there were no landmarks to see any more . . . I didn't want anyone to notice me crying.

On the hill we had made solid progress and I realized I could no longer see the campsite, which had disappeared into the now hidden valley floor. We sat on the grass alongside a drystone wall and drank in the setting. This was the most beautiful place I had ever seen. After an hour we were so high the fells of the western Lakes were laid out on the horizon. To our right the northern fells climbed higher still into the blue sky, which acted as a fast conveyor belt to numerous fat white clouds. If we climbed much further I would be able to touch one.

Bleachy (whose hair went white in the sun) and Dickie (real name Richard) were jumping around between the large flat slates that were scattered on the steep hillside. There was a lot more animal shit to avoid here compared to Eltham Park. Bleachy had perfected the art of lobbing a stone into a pile of the stuff, causing all in the vicinity to dive for cover to avoid being freckled. I turned one of the stones on its side and rolled it away from me, but the steepness of the hill caused it to stay upright and gather pace. 'Oh shit!' someone said. We watched on as the large stone disc began accelerating down the mountainside. Far below a sheep ambled into line with the tumbling round slate and we held our breath. At the last moment the slate hit a small lump just in front of the sheep, and bounced up suddenly, clearing the sheep's white woolly coat by inches before clattering into another drystone wall further down the mountain. The laughter that followed was more in relief that we hadn't decapitated the sheep. No more stone rolling happened after that.

There was a growing rumble to the right, like the sound of distant thunder. Two black shapes appeared on the horizon, moving impossibly fast towards us. In a second or two they were upon us; a pair of RAF fighter jets thundered down the valley. As they reached us they dipped quickly in height so that we were able to look across at them. They were so close I saw the silhouette of the pilot in his cockpit. My chest felt the vibration of the ground-shaking roar of the engines as they passed, ridiculously loud, and getting lower still. How could they not crash? How could they fly so fast? The aircraft turned sharply through the valley, the hills now above them on either side, and began to bank steadily downwards as they headed lower still towards a large expanse of water in the distance. In a moment they were gone, but the rumble of their thunder faded more gradually. I was on my feet, jumping up and down, cheering, but when I realized no one else was, I quickly sat down again.

'Where are they going, Bear?' I asked, in a fast and excited voice.

'Dunno,' he replied calmly. 'They do that a lot here. You'll see 'em all week, provided it ain't rainin' – but it's usually rainin'.' Bear was less excited by the whole event, but he'd been here before.

'What's that big lake over there?' I asked.

'That's Windermere, durr-brain.'

I gulped. It was vast even from here, and I could only see some of it from our perch on the mountainside. At least the RAF were around in case anything went wrong. The Senior squad had come here for one reason – to train for swimming the Channel. Lake Windermere was very cold and the swimming conditions were hostile. There was no better place to prepare, according to John.

The rain arrived later that afternoon, and it didn't stop. The July daylight began to fade, already darkened by the heavy clouds above. The stream next to our camp began to rush and swell – the only possible escape for the mass of water that was now falling between the mountains that defined the valley. Our camp was to be tested.

In the boys' tent, my sleeping bag had again been rolled out for me at the far end, as far away from John as it could be. The entrances to all the tents were now strewn with large white pads called 'incontinence sheets', which had somehow been acquired from the local hospital. I did not understand their medical purpose as I didn't know what incontinence meant, but they were clearly very good at soaking up the mud and water that were already starting to make living conditions difficult.

When it rained there was another rule to the campsite. 'Don't touch the tent,' John would bark. It was a bad idea to break the rule on two counts. Firstly I had seen at Dover that touching the inside caused the fabric of the tent to lose its waterproof effect. The rain would seep in through the canvas in rivulets, rather than run down the outside in the way that reminded me of the ducks in Eltham Park. Secondly, if John or a Senior swimmer saw the offence, 'the ladle' would be mentioned. The food tent was home to two ladles. One had holes in it, the other was smooth. It was a source of debate as to which one was better to be whacked with. I was in the 'holes are better' camp on account of there being less surface metal to injure the victim. Others, like Tetley (who, thanks to his dog-ear-shaped specs, looked like the cartoon tea man from the TV advert), claimed that holes could only *increase* the speed of travel, resulting in a heftier clout. Thus the flat ladle was preferable for the offender. Physics, apparently.

Dinner in the food tent that first night was taken in silence, less for the constant hammering of the rain on the canvas above than because the group had not rested since the 2 a.m. meet in Eltham, a forgotten universe. John sat on one of three deckchairs, lined up on one side of the tent like thrones, and placed so as to look over the rest of us who sat on the tent floor, cold but happily still dry. Tinned minced beef, mash and tinned processed marrowfat peas on the menu. I had learned to like this meal in Dover and, much to Anna's disbelief, normally asked for seconds, despite being the smallest. There was a pudding too, of tinned Ambrosia creamed rice, with a spoonful of sweet Robinson's jam plopped in the middle.

John's chair was nearest the wire food rack, and the ladles. The other two chairs were reserved for the most senior of Seniors: Mother Duck (who had prepared the food) and, on this occasion, Tetley. In the days to come, the third chair would be reserved for the swimmer in most need. This was yet to mean anything to me, but then I had never tried to swim Lake Windermere.

I gulped down the creamed rice, happy not to be told off for being fussy, like those who were ordered to clean their bowls. I still felt nervous. A couple of the girls wore the same t-shirt that instructed everyone to 'RELAX', but I was finding this quite hard, despite rehearsals in Dover. Everything felt new again in this wild place. Thankfully, Anna was sitting next to me, so I helped her finish her rice pudding when no one was looking. As we sat in silence, far from home, I suddenly longed for the safety of Eltham, school, Rat-Bag and Miss Morgan. Just two weeks ago I had won my 25 metre swimming badge in

Miss Morgan's final lesson. It had been easy and didn't feel like an achievement. More to the point, it was utterly useless up here, in the North.

The next morning I was awoken by shouting. I could hear John outside, barking orders at people. I had slept well but could feel a warm dampness under my body. I thought I had wet my sleeping bag and began to panic. If the elder boys found out, I would be in big trouble. Bleachy and I looked around the tent, which was now mostly empty. I said nothing, hoping to cover my shame somehow, and followed Bleachy outside.

The stream was now an angry river and had burst its banks. The bubbling clear water had been replaced by a grey-brown torrent, sweeping its way through the campsite, rushing up towards the girls' tent. The girls, including Anna to my relief, had been evacuated in their pyjamas, and were watching on from inside the food tent. John, wearing a vest and rolled up trousers, was frantically trying to untie guy lines and remove the big wooden stakes with a mallet. Bear, Mother Duck, Tetley, Panda and Palfrey held the frame of the large tent as he did so. Within a few moments the entire structure was unhitched, lifted clear of both the waterline and the contents of the tent within, and moved a few paces uphill. The girls rushed from the food tent, grabbed the groundsheet, which held their sleeping bags and possessions, and dragged it back under the frame of the relocated tent. The panic subsided and people began to laugh and cheer. John beamed a smile. 'That was fuckin' close!' he said triumphantly. 'Still, could have been worse . . . at least it wasn't the boys' tent.'

Further down the valley all hell had broken loose. Many tents were flooded and some were being dragged away by the river. Traumatized holidaymakers sat in their cars trying to warm up and consider their options. Children could be heard crying. I looked up. The storm had passed and the morning sky was a fresh bright blue. I realized I had not wet the bed after all, but that my sleeping bag was on the edge of the tent and so had less protection from the rain and condensation. I was so relieved I decided to say nothing about it. I would lay the sleeping bag out in a way that might allow it to dry off; tents got very hot when the sun was out. It was the same reason why we never left Flossie in the car in summer. Perhaps I had also found *another* new use for the big white pads; maybe I would hide one under my sleeping bag, I thought, pleased with my ingenuity. The cars of the displaced began their slow exit procession through the emptying campsite. It still felt very early. For some reason John allowed no one bar himself to wear a watch. He gave another order. 'Kettle on! Breakfast is late . . .'

For a moment no one moved . . .

'Bloody get on with it then!'

Things got moving in earnest on the Monday as John set in motion a punishing schedule of relay swims and solo attempts on the length of the lake with his Senior swimmers. The schedule was secret – no one knew who would swim on any given day – and I wondered if John even knew himself or whether he made up his mind as his head hit the pillow (the only pillow allowed in the boys' tent) late each evening, in a state of physical exhaustion.

We woke on the Monday to find John had already left, along with Shovel, Bear and Tetley. Any one of them could have been the swimmer, with the other two there to row the boat and act in support. Everyone else had been left in camp. Mother Duck took charge, which was good news as there was much to be done. There was breakfast to cook – the same every day: porridge, followed by beans and scrambled eggs with white bread, and tea, always lots of tea. Then there was washing-up to be avoided, especially on days where the eggs and porridge had been burned badly on the base of the huge shiny cooking pots. We would all have a wash in the communal ablutions next to the washing-up block. I was admired for the double-sided yellow bath mitt Mum had thoughtfully packed.

Dennis seemed to appear every morning after breakfast from nowhere, which meant it was time to go, and, once loaded, the bus came alive with pop music. Miss Piggy had recorded the charts on Radio 1 the Sunday before, which was apparently a tradition. There were always clunky links between songs, where the DJ's voice came in over the top, before jumping to the next tune. With a few other favourite tracks thrown in, the tape was a full ninety minute time capsule of the summer of 1985, and it rarely fell silent.

The charts were a big deal. 'Frankie', by Sister Sledge, was number one and the girls loved it, so it became the theme tune of the week. Within a day or two we all knew every word and sang in unison as we journeyed up and down the 10 mile lake to the next rendezvous. The Eurythmics were threatening to topple 'Frankie' from the top spot with 'There Must Be an Angel'. Madonna, Kool & the Gang and Marillion were among many others. Occasionally, the boys would insist on something cooler, and so *Techno 1* – a compilation album of computerish music – would be heard for a while, before the girls vetoed it for 'being weird' and went back to 'Frankie'.

As the week unfolded I began to understand the routine: breakfast, minibus trips and pop soundtrack, swimming, and then more swimming. But on that Monday I didn't know what to expect. Getting changed for breakfast in the boys' tent with the others, I rummaged through my kit bag looking for a fresh pair of pants. They were proving hard to find even though I didn't have many clothes with me. I realized that there were fewer pairs of pants than I had expected. Only three in fact, and since one already had skid-marks, that left just two pairs for the whole week. Even my poor maths allowed me to compute that I was likely to end up with no clean pants by Wednesday, and if that happened it would be a catastrophe. I hunkered down in the tent hoping no one was watching me, and began to panic. Others left for the food tent and I was alone. Another feeling took over; like panic, but mixed with a loss of some kind. I felt my face go red and I began to cry. I heard Mother Duck from the food tent . . . 'Erm, where is Young Thomas?' she demanded. 'I'll go,' called out Panda. I was about to be discovered. There was nowhere to hide.

Panda's real name was Graham. Anna said that as a Senior swimmer he was in training for a possible solo attempt of the Channel. He was called Panda because he tanned easily in the water, and so after a long swim the skin around his eyes was whiter than the rest of his face, thanks to the goggles. He was one of the biggest in the group, tall and broad. He had a wide smile, framed by a large friendly face. I guessed he must have been about fifteen years old. He appeared in the entrance of the boys' tent and fought his way over the mass of bags to reach me before sitting down alongside. He had a deep voice – a man's voice. 'What's wrong, little man?' he said.

'I don't know,' I said – mostly a lie given I had now discovered the pants shortage. I also knew my bottom lip was making an 'r' shape and that I couldn't make it go back to normal.

'Well, did you know that John has asked me, *personally*, to look after you?'

I looked up at him, tears still budding in my eyes, but offering no reply.

'. . . to look out for you, and make sure you are OK,' Panda added.

'No?' I sniffed, as if asking him a question.

'Well, he has, so it will all be fine,' he said in a low reassuring tone. 'I think . . .' he paused, 'I think you might just be a bit *homesick.*'

I thought about this. I didn't remember ever being diagnosed with homesickness – I normally just got tonsillitis – so was not sure how it would feel even if I was. 'Maybe,' I said. Gradually my downturned lip returned to normal, possibly on account of the medical diagnosis.

'Well, the good news is that homesickness can be cured,' carried on Panda. 'You just need to think of other things, and keep busy.' I didn't offer a reply to this either. I already knew we would be busy. Panda put his big arm around my shoulders and said nothing for a moment. We sat there in the tent for a minute in silence. Then Panda stood up, picked up my small swim bag from among the pile and headed out of the boys' tent. 'Come on!' he said, smiling. I followed him, wiping the tears away, hoping no one would notice I had been crying. In the food tent everyone was tucking into porridge. Mother Duck handed me a bowl as I walked in. She winked at me, and I went and sat next to Anna, who studied me briefly before offering the very faintest of smiles. My plastic plate of scrambled eggs, beans and bread arrived. A few minutes after that I asked for seconds. Maybe the worst of the homesickness had passed already.

The CB cracked back with the loud *chhhhhhhcchh* as Dennis let go of the mic. But there was still no reply. Dennis adjusted the dials again. 'JB, JB, this is Menace, do you read me, OVER!' he repeated. *Chhhhcchh.* Still nothing.

'Let me 'av a go,' said Cynthia, his wife.

'JB, JB, this is Snowball . . . Av you got yer' boots on, over?' *Chhhhhchhh.*

Cynthia, whose handle was a reference to her favourite drink, gave Dennis a look that I could not decode. We listened in silence. There was no music playing now. The only noise was the rain drumming incessantly on the roof of the minibus.

After a long pause, John's voice crackled back at us from somewhere on the lake, breaking the tense hush. *'Snowball, this is JB, JB . . .'* I looked around at the others smiling excitedly, amazed . . . *'Reading you loud and clear. How am I back, over?'* John had been reminded by Cynthia to flick on the power booster – his 'boots' – to his CB rig, which was now on the rowing boat and powered by a car battery. He was out there somewhere, in the boat and the squall, with Tetley, Bear and Shovel.

Our bus was filled with a combustible mix of fear and excitement, for someone who wasn't even there – the swimmer. He or she was trying to conquer the lake, end to end, in one long swim. Windermere was vast, 10.5 miles long, and cold, especially in early summer. Water temperature was key. Windermere was colder than the Channel at this time of year according to John, and after a snowy winter and cool spring the temperature remained in the mid to low 50 degrees Fahrenheit, or between 12 and 15 degrees Celsius. The bus was parked in a lay-by, an elevated spot halfway up the steep-sided valley on the west of the lake. We looked out of the windows of the bus through the heavy rain, wiping away the condensation inside the glass. From this distance, even from this vantage point, trying to locate a 12 foot rowing boat within the immense expanse of the lake – or the few miles of it we could see – was not easy. But there were very few vantage points to choose from. Unable to locate the boat and swimmer, a sense of collective nervousness had begun to build.

'Got him,' said Dennis, who had the advantage of a set of binoculars. The doors of the bus flew open and we ran out into the rain to get a better look, passing the binoculars between us. When it was my turn I needed some directing, but after a while, there, within the magnified jerky view of the lenses, was a rowing boat. I saw three people, one rowing from the middle, the others sitting at the stern. They wore luminous orange waterproofs with hoods, matching the trademark orange swimming cap worn by club swimmers. Blue and white flags flew from poles at each end of the boat – stiff in the wind, in spite of the rain that would have long since soaked them. On the near side of the boat I noticed a rhythmic *splash, splash, splash*, and a flash of colour, orange again, amid the water, which was grey, reflecting the sky above it. The swimmer, whoever it was, was still in – after about five hours. Collective nervousness was replaced by collective sympathy.

I had been for my first swim in Lake Windermere that morning. We swam in the rain from a pretty shoreline on the north edge of the lake. The shelters in the pleasaunce park at Ambleside were empty. Just like at Dover, we seemed to do things when everyone else preferred to stay indoors. The destination that morning had been a flotilla of cruising boats that were bobbing quietly on their mooring buoys out in the deep water of the north shore. Maybe 100 metres in each direction, I reckoned. This swimming was a different physical experience to the sea or the pool. The visibility of the water was exciting; I could see the plants, weeds and stones below – until the water got too deep. In the shallows there were thousands of tiny fish in big shoals, darting all over the place. They scattered in all directions with incredible speed once my foot entered the water. I wondered if I would see a big fish. The water was clean and clear – no salt, and no chlorine either. It was cold, and wonderful. And the colder the water was, the more I was on terms with the older swimmers. Many of them became cold quicker than me and so reached their limit before I needed to get out. I had good resilience, I was just not as fast.

Back in the lay-by, John reported that Shovel was expected to make it to Ambleside in one to two hours' time. She was tired and slowing, having already put 7.5 miles of the lake behind her in terrible conditions. I knew myself from Dover that she was not one for giving in – especially to cold. She was normally one of the last ones out, along with Mother Duck and Miss Piggy, and, like them, rarely shivered let alone boasted. The bus headed for Ambleside for the second time that day. I thought of Shovel out in the middle of the huge lake and hoped she was OK. Not too cold, not too tired. But in truth we all knew she must have been both of those things and was likely to be suffering. The longest I had managed in Dover harbour was about thirty minutes, possibly a mile of back and forth swimming if I was lucky. I was beginning to discover that things were not really measured by distance; what mattered was endurance. Time was relevant, but only in the context of someone's ability to withstand the conditions. As time passes, so fades the swimmer's ability to survive the cold and continue the physical motion of swimming. A mental challenge evolves in parallel to the physical one. At some point a moment is reached where the journey ends; either because the swimmer cannot continue, or, hopefully, because they have reached the shore. Shovel had no one to beat but herself. It didn't matter how long it took her to complete the distance – just completing the distance was the point. I had never seen anyone do something so remarkable. Could she really swim all that way?

A small crowd began to grow on the shore. The rain had stopped and so the passers-by and holidaymakers had ventured out again from the shops, guesthouses and B&Bs. The rowing boat was only a couple of hundred metres off, still clearly marked by the blue and white flags. We had tracked it from half a mile out, anxious to see the splashing that would confirm Shovel was still in the water. I saw John at the back, wearing his distinctive blue and white woolly bobble hat, and caught his shouts of encouragement on the wind. Shovel's strokes were slow, laboured and deliberate – the oar strokes required to keep up with her were occasional and delicate. As she edged towards shore she stopped, approached a large orange boating buoy, swam up and kissed it. I looked at Anna in confusion – she shrugged her shoulders. In the final few yards of this slow-motion drama, she stopped again, and instead of resuming with the front crawl that had carried her 10.5 miles through the wind and rain, began to swim butterfly – in a heavy and defiant rhythm . . . until she touched land.

As she staggered ashore the bemused onlookers began to clap. The water ran off her bare, broad shoulders in large beads as she knelt in the shallows and began to scramble forwards. The remains of the grease that had covered her seven hours earlier were still visible. Her swimming costume was a saggy mess, and her face . . . her face looked very different: puffy and swollen, with a grim expression. As Shovel struggled to her feet the rowing boat behind her sped up quickly on both oars; momentum was needed to gain a holding on the shore, and the wooden hull made a muffled rattling sound as it collided with the shingle at some pace. Shovel fell back to her knees, before standing again. Wobbling, she took three deliberate and careful steps up the beach, and sat down, exhausted. At that point the swimmers joined in the celebration, clapping and cheering along with the watching public. In a moment John was on the beach, looking into Shovel's eyes, holding both of her hands out in front of her, asking her quiet questions. It reminded me of a boxer being spoken to by his trainer between rounds – like I had seen on the telly. Shovel sat motionless, before slowly removing her goggles and looking around her, smiling broadly but as if half asleep.

The tourists' cameras clicked. John helped Shovel to her feet and began what looked like a mummification process, wrapping each of her limbs in the big incontinence pads before zipping her into a body bag, presumably also acquired from the hospital. She was carried in a fireman's lift onto our minibus by Panda. With Dennis at the wheel our bus sped away. The week-long conquest of England's longest lake, by John Bullet's team of swimmers from South-East London, had begun.

I watched the bus disappear and turned to see Palfrey, now in a pair of trunks, standing motionless in a star shape on the beach. John, wearing a pair of funny blue gloves, began to apply thick white grease all over his body. Palfrey looked nervous but masked his apprehension with a smile as he was photographed by the tourists who watched on with still more fascination. Tetley and John were joined by Tanya on the rowing boat, which we pushed out into deep water with a team effort. I watched Palfrey set off, still enthralled by what I had just witnessed. A major achievement, by Shovel, had just occurred, but there was clearly no time to waste on group celebrations. John was heading south now, with another swimmer, for a second solo attempt in the same day. I gulped at the prospect of ever being asked to do that myself. Not in a million years, I thought. The boat and swimmer moved slowly out into the lake, John's hat distinctive against the Lakeland backdrop and grey skies. It was just after lunchtime.

'Right, come on, you lot!' called out Mother Duck, once the boat was 200 metres offshore. 'Let's go for another swim.'

The third chair in the food tent that night was for Palfrey. Shovel sat in the middle chair and seemed almost back to her normal self. John sat in his usual chair – nearest the ladles. Palfrey was still cold, wrapped in multiple layers of clothing, and was having trouble speaking, but I didn't think he wanted to say much anyway as I sat watching, cross-legged on the floor of the tent. Tinned ravioli, mash and tinned marrowfat peas arrived on a plastic plate. I didn't ask for seconds that night.

Information had been scarce and whispered. With John out of sight and Palfrey being showered, Mother Duck explained that he had been pulled out of the lake 2 miles from the hamlet of Lakeside, towards the southern end, after about 8 miles and four to five hours of swimming. He had swum quickly to Belle Isle – the 4.5 mile point – and then further, down the longer and narrower stretch past a place called Storrs Temple, but was eventually unable to carry on. He had become very, very cold. None of us were there to see the boat land with him in it. I didn't know how they got him out and kept him safe, or how he got back to the campsite, but he was here, and he had the special chair. I wondered what would happen in the morning, and who would be next. Then I remembered something else. I was down to my last pair of pants.

Friday arrived and it was still raining. It had rained just about all week and I was used to it by now. Swimming had become my cure for homesickness, as if the cold water was itself the medicine. Miss Piggy had swum the lake's length, not for the first time, and with some ease. Mother Duck and Panda had made the distance, while Palfrey, Bear and Big Steve were all pulled out. The relay teams then had their turn, swimming sections of the lake in groups of three or four, an hour at a time, sharing the rowing duties on the boat. Every day, *Swan* and *Teal*, the lake's own veteran passenger steamers, plied the length of the lake, from Ambleside to Lakeside and back again, and so did we, waving at the passengers from the water or the old wooden boat. The chain ferry at Belle Isle clanked its way back and forth as we swam around the network of small islands in the vicinity, passing the time between solo attempt rendezvous and mealtimes. The stereo on the bus ran out of batteries twice, requiring a whip-round for change to ensure the mix tape never fell silent. We ate porridge, drank soup and swam. My towel was never dry.

That final morning, I stood on the remote lake shore with Bleachy, and pulled my goggles on over my now well-worn orange hat. This was the final event of the swimming week for us all – a mile sprint across the widest part of the lake. The width event. I could see the shoreline a mile off but couldn't tell where we would need to aim for. The shore looked so far away, even as the mountains behind continued to dominate the scene. At my back, the green forest looked on in silence, dripping rain that carried the scent of the watching pine trees. In front of me the rowing boat held its station in deeper water, 'oars-in' to reduce drift against the wind and choppy wavelets. The boat was less crowded now. John and Tetley had rowed us over the widest part of Windermere on two sets of oars in order for us then to swim back.

We were both nervous, but Bleachy was perhaps more so, even though he was older (the same age as Anna) and much faster. He knew the cold was harder on him, being skinny, and the lake was about 57 degrees Fahrenheit (13 degrees Celsius) at this, the widest point. I reminded myself that everyone else had made it over already. Palfrey had probably broken a speed record, and I knew Anna had made it, as had both cousins. But that all just meant I couldn't be the one to fail, and neither could Bleachy. We were the last boat.

Then I remembered something else. If I could swim this mile, further and colder than anything so far, then I would be with Dad, Mum and Flossie, who were waiting for me on the opposite shoreline. It wasn't at all clear why they had arrived in the Lake District, but I knew I needed to be with them again in the shortest time possible – probably about forty minutes given the wind.

'Ready, mate?' said Bleachy, in a tone that confirmed his apprehension.

'Ready, Bleachy,' I replied, keeping my eyes fixed on the rowing boat without looking back at him.

We walked purposefully into the clear Lakeland water side by side. I had learned from Bleachy the best way to get in was with purpose . . . the water was so cold here there was no other way.

After what felt like about twenty minutes I could not keep up with the boat and my arms and shoulders were starting to hurt. Bleachy was bobbing in the water, waiting for me, getting cold. Looking up every few strokes to see where he and the boat were just made me more tired. But if I didn't look up I couldn't see which direction to swim in, which was frightening. And without the boat I was in the middle on my own. I wondered how far we had come. I was starting to feel cold too – a warning sign. I knew the water in the middle was colder than on the shores – just the day before I had managed nearly a full thirty minutes on a relay swim in the southern part of the lake with Anna, Shovel, Miss Piggy, Bleachy and the cousins. Anna was embarrassed by having to put her arm around Bleachy in the rowing boat to help him warm up after his stint. John had repeatedly explained that human body contact was the best way to warm up a cold swimmer.

It felt like a long time since we had left the other side and we had clearly made progress – but how much? Then a new thought – what if I didn't make it? . . . not good enough, and the only one? I looked up to the front to see that the boat had stopped rowing again. Maybe this was the moment John would pull me out for being too slow. I swam as hard as I could to catch up. When I got there John was shouting at Bleachy to keep going. He was shivering in the water and complaining of the cold.

'You're nearly there, lad!' shouted John. 'Stop your complaining. Now kick out more and just get on with it.'

Bleachy did not reply.

Tetley let the oars rest in their rowlocks and moved to the back of the rowing boat, where a kind of open boot in the stern allowed a cold swimmer to be pulled aboard should it be deemed necessary.

John steadied the oars. I felt guilty. Bleachy was so cold because he kept having to stop, to wait for me. John looked down at me from the boat, oars now in hand. 'All right, let's go, Young Thomas. You need to speed up now, lad. Less than half a mile left.'

He bent right forwards, arms outstretched to gain a full swing for the oars, which pointed forwards of the boat – ready to be recovered with a big heavy pull. As the oars splashed into the water under the ever-grey sky John heaved, letting out an unscripted rallying cry as he did so: 'Let's go! . . . Go! . . . GO!' The boat gathered speed.

I began to calm down. Now I was alongside the boat I could see John on every stroke, and the faster pace felt manageable. Out in front Bleachy was pushing ahead, striking for the shore, which was finally looking closer. Every breath looked the same above the water; John's eyes studying mine from beneath the blue and white bobble hat, an unflinching gaze on his weathered face – almost a look of curiosity. John looked tough, as though he belonged here, in total control, which made me feel safe. I also became aware, perhaps for the first time, that I was desperate not to let him down. Beneath the surface, each dip of the oar left a swirling arc of bubbles trailing behind the blade. I glimpsed their fizzing and rising pattern with each breath and became slowly hypnotized by the repetition. 'Frankie' started playing inside my head, and so I sang along to myself.

The cold was taking a hold on me – numbing my senses. It was my first proper experience of the steady degradation that cold water causes, given enough time – where thoughts become slower, and where the core of the body gradually adjusts to its setting, trying to maintain the essentials by triggering involuntary shivering. I kept singing until I got bored of the song, and decided to replace 'Frankie' with a day-dream about Miss Piggy. Other key moments of the week began to replay in my mind. I let them play. It was the best distraction I had found.

I knew already that the days leading up to this final event had been special, and I didn't even have to go home yet. I had slowly begun to feel part of this new world, having spent day after day splashing and swimming in the cold clean Lakeland water, while the fells, their sheep, forests and crags stood silently watching over us. I had discovered hidden places. Windermere's more remote shores were always deserted, its secret islands sometimes the only protection from the weather, which could become brutal very quickly. Then there was camping, skimming stones, CB radios and pop music. The group looked after each other like the best kind of family from morning till night, and I was now one of their number. Total immersion.

I was still quite raw about the conclusion of the pants incident. On the Thursday afternoon Mum and Dad had arrived without notice and found our group in Ambleside, waiting for a swimmer – Panda on that day – to complete his length. Blessed with the week's only sunshine, he was even more Panda-like after six hours in the lake. The relief I felt was not at seeing Mum and Dad, but because Dad was in a position to solve the pants issue without anyone ever finding out. I tasked him with purchasing some immediately – no questions, no objections.

That evening, I was handed a brown paper bag by Dennis at the campsite. I peeked inside and my heart sank; the bag contained the worst pants I could ever have been forced to wear. They were the Y-front type from the old days, which only dads wore. They were bad enough to earn me a full barrage of derision at school, if I was ever stupid enough to wear them on PE day. The material was a brownish flowery paisley pattern, like some of Dad's older ties, and there was dark yellow furry piping dividing the segments of the 'Y'. I wandered behind the wash block in a panic. I checked over my shoulder that there was no one around, and held a pair up in front of me, hoping that some magic would change the contents of the bag at the second time of opening. How could he get this so wrong? The other pair were the same style but with an even worse colour scheme of light blue with yellow swirls and brown furry piping. I stuffed them back in the paper bag and considered my options. Concealment was the only strategy.

Back on the tent pitch John was making a cup of tea on the camping stove – on his own for once as all the others headed off to wash up and then swim in the mountain stream before the sun went down. 'What's in the bag, Young Thomas?' he asked as I walked in.

'Nothing, John,' I said, panicking, 'nothing at all.'

'Really? Nothing at all, eh?'

I paused. I trusted John, even though he was very strict and scary, or maybe because of this. Perhaps I would *half* let him into the secret. After all, he alone could protect me from the others if the pants were ever discovered. With a serious face, I began to explain. 'The contents of this bag, John, are quite personal. I would like it very much if you would not look inside the bag, or say anything at all about the bag, to anyone. Anyone at all.'

He looked back at me with his usual hard gaze and studied me, frowning a little.

'OK, Young Thomas. I *promise* . . . not to look inside your paper bag, or even to mention the paper bag, to *anyone*. Anyone *at all*.'

'Thank you, John,' I replied and couldn't help smiling at the relief. He smiled back. With just the two of us there in the tent,

I felt safer and more at home. I tucked the brown bag out of sight, between a couple of large tins of baked beans on the food rack, and went to sit down, hoping I might get to talk more to John. Perhaps he would tell me more about swimming, about himself, or a story of the great lake and Channel swims of the past. He sat in his deckchair, tea in hand. Only John had a china mug. His eyes began to close for a moment, before he jolted himself awake, but it happened again. I said nothing from the far corner. He began to snore quietly. In the distance I could hear the others laughing and splashing in the stream, the sound carrying clearly in the twilight of the campsite. Sheep somewhere on the fell cried out intermittently. Nowhere sounded like this place.

'Sound travels at night,' John mumbled, half asleep. He was fond of saying this in a stage whisper once it got dark. Before long it would be time for tea, a biscuit and bed. The Tilley lamp would be lit in the food tent and the swimmers would gather around it before going to sleep. Jokes would be told. Someone would fart loudly before attempting to claim innocence. Any large insect unfortunate enough to enter the tent might become an experiment in burn-time on the surface of the lamp. The week was nearly over.

Dennis popped his head cheerily around the door of the tent and startled John awake. 'JB, I gave Young Thomas those pants . . . Just so you know.' I sighed to myself.

'Bugger off,' replied John, before closing his eyes again.

'A hundred metres to go!' John shouted at me. 'Stay with the fuckin' boat!' I was jolted back into the present very suddenly. I looked up, and could just make out a crowd of people on the lake shore. Bleachy was already there. And then finally, after what felt like an age, I was too.

Dad's hug was different to normal – urgent almost. He

swept me up in his arms before I could even take the three steps – the three unaided steps on dry land that meant I had completed my first solo open water swim. I felt his rough beard on my bare shoulders as he carried me to the kit bags, assembled swimmers and a pile of warm dry towels. He smiled. I shivered violently.

'Thanks for coming up, Dad,' I said with quivering lips as he rubbed my body vigorously with a rough towel in an attempt to warm me up. Flossie barked around my feet, jumping up and down in her excitement.

'Well done, son. Well done,' said Dad.

'We will always be here when you need us,' he added.

Soon after, Mum and Dad disappeared again, along with a few other parents, including Uncle John, who had also popped up from nowhere that morning, and within an hour or two all the swimmers were in Bowness on an end of week shopping trip. I had £2 left of my £5 pocket money. I felt wonderful after completing my swim: I'd let no one down and was sure I was part of the group, even if I didn't have a nickname yet. The tourist shops were full of colourful gifts, trinkets, shortbread and Kendal Mint Cake. I bought Mum and Dad a little glass with a tiny painted map of Lake Windermere on it. They would like that, and probably put it in the special glass cabinet once at home. At 90 pence this was quite an outlay so I kept the other pound note in reserve for the journey back, in case I got hungry. I decided to buy a quarter of sherbet lemons with the remaining 10 pence and went off in search of a sweet shop, before discovering Anna shortly afterwards.

'Hi Anna. Look at this . . . For Mum and Dad!' I announced proudly.

'Hi Tomsk . . . very nice!' she replied, using a name from the Wombles she often preferred to my own.

'I still can't believe they were there to see us swim the mile.'

Anna didn't reply this time, but was clearly masking a slight smile as she looked away. Dad's words from the landing point came back to me and I opened my eyes wide in a moment of discovery.

'It was you, wasn't it.'

Again no reply, just a wider smile this time as she looked back at me fondly.

It turned out Anna had used the payphone at the campsite to call home earlier in the week at a point where she felt I might not cope. I reached into the pocket of my shorts for the heavy 10 pence piece, before remembering I had just spent it on sweets.

'It's OK, Tomsk. You can pay me back,' she smiled, reading my mind. I held out the little white paper bag and I offered her the first sherbet lemon. The first one out of the bag always tasted best.

3. *Summertime*

7.15 a.m., 6 September 1988 – 2 hours, 4.5 miles off the French coast, English Channel

The sun was almost blinding, refracting its morning rays into a white haze through the grease that I had accidentally smeared on my goggles. My right eye was a fraction higher in the water when taking a breath, but the effect of the sun was worse as the lens carried more grease. I knew when I put on the goggles back on the dark French beach that I had made a mistake, but I hadn't foreseen this. It was dazzling, uncomfortable and it made me lose my bearings, especially in relation to the boat, which was the only constant reference point in the moving sea. If I got closer to the boat, I could take advantage of her shadow and avoid the sun, but if I did that the diesel fumes from the marine engine exhaust were much stronger and made me feel sick. I was not allowed to touch the boat nor anyone on board for the entire swim, else the swim would be abandoned at that moment. The rules were strict, hence the presence on board of an observer from the Channel Swimming Association, and I wasn't about to chance it. The risk of being washed into the boat, or simply swimming into her in an absent moment, was too great.

What was confusing was why the sun was in my eyes at all. I thought I'd be swimming away from it, swimming west. But I was facing into it on a right-hand breath when I looked behind me, so I must be swimming north. Or at least north-west. I had a habit of breathing slightly 'behind' me, as if trying to speak into my armpit (it was useful to do this in heavy weather to avoid gulping in water), so everything I could see was probably offset by more than 90 degrees to my body. I was probably 'looking backwards' at things while swimming away from them at the same time. I sighted the bows and port side of a large ferry coming out of Calais, which confirmed things – the ferry was taking a more direct route. Swimming on my current course I would eventually cross its track, although it would long since have motored past me. I wondered how long the wash of the huge vessel would take to reach me, and if it would be fun when it arrived – like a wave machine.

Given England was due west of Calais and over my left shoulder, our direction could only be because of the tide. According to John, the currents off the French coast were especially strong, the headland at Calais acting as a slingshot to the mass of water heading north for six hours and then south for the six after that. This was one factor that accounted for so many failures among swimmers who chose to set out from England. Some people thought that swimming from France was easier as a result, although I wondered if the Dover and Kent coast tides could really be any different for getting ashore. Regardless of the direction of travel, more than 3,000 people had attempted this in the past, though fewer than 300 had ever made it. John had once spoken of a small current that could push you off the French coast, towards England for a while, if only it could be found. Assuming this was the plan, we must have failed to find it if I was heading north-west. As to being easier, well, nothing about this swim felt very easy so far.

To be hand-railing the French coast felt like a very long route to take. If only I could get further out into the middle then maybe the currents would be less, and I could just swim west. Maybe I was trapped in a stream of water heading the wrong way. I sped up for a while. Perhaps we could find the friendly current, I thought. Then 'FOLLOW THE FUCKIN'

BOAT, TEFAL' rang in my head – a lesson learned on Windermere. Trust Willy, I thought. He knew which way to head. Willy's job as pilot was to set the course that maximized the chances of success for the swimmer. He would be getting a constant flow of information from John – my expected average speed, and the rate of deterioration caused by fatigue – and then applying his real knowledge of tidal direction and speed to the situation at hand. Good pilots were like gold dust, and, according to Anna, John only ever used Willy.

The excitement of the night swim faded, giving way to a nagging feeling. These were the early hours. I could see France a few miles behind me on every breath. I knew that by far the greater part of the swim still lay ahead. I was not even halfway – not even close. Probably not even a quarter, bearing in mind I had not yet stopped for a chocolate biscuit or spoken to John from the water since we left France. The nagging feeling gnawed away. How was this possible? How could I expect to effectively double my best and longest ever swim on Windermere (of 15.5 miles in seven and a quarter hours), at the very first time of asking and in the English Channel? I knew that I could do things at my age that other people could not. But my implied one in ten chance was slim, even in the best of conditions. The anxiety built slowly. Eventually it became fear. Without a release valve, fear soon tends to become panic.

'Calm down, settle in . . . (Recover leading arm, exhale.) Calm down, settle in . . . (Recover leading arm, exhale),' I repeated to myself out loud underwater. Maybe for twenty strokes or more. I realized that mentally I had been here before. The scale of the challenge had gripped me. My mind stepped back, to the moments and the swims, especially those on Windermere, that had brought me here; into the middle, with John, somewhere off France on what looked to be a bright sunny morning. This was just fear. Nothing more. I decided to find another way to pass the time.

I looked at the crew of the boat with renewed interest on every breath for a while. Breakfast was being served. People were busily moving around the deck, a couple of them holding sandwiches. Bacon sandwiches? My favourite. Cups of tea were handed out. 'Fuckers' – I heard my own voice underwater. I had discovered that sometimes it helped to make sounds while breathing out to keep myself company. I'd hear my words inside my head but also as if from an underwater speaker. John Callaway, the assistant coach, appeared on the rail and leaned over to communicate with me visually, as I inhaled on every stroke. He was dressed in an immaculate soft tracksuit that had 'Canada' printed across the front and patches embroidered on the arms. JC never looked scruffy. He seemed in high spirits as he beamed at me. I grinned back. But taking a breath made this hard, so I threw an arm high instead, half swim, half wave, as a kind of acknowledgement. It worked and he gave me the thumbs up sign, accompanied by a quizzical face. He was asking me if I was OK. In response I 'dolphined' down on my front crawl stroke to indicate things were fine and looked up for his reply on the subsequent breath. He just smiled at me, hands now clasped in front of him. Our line of communication was open.

JC stayed on the rail for a while, keeping me company though we could not speak. I enjoyed this while it lasted. It was sometimes enough just to look at someone, and have them look back at you. At one point he pulled a lollipop out of his pocket, unwrapped it dramatically, and made exaggerated faces of joy and satisfaction as he sucked on the thing. He knew I liked Chupa Chups lollipops, and had clearly brought a whole bag of them with him, just to tease me. I shook my head in the normal way to register my disapproval. The teasing, which had been perfected over three years on Lake Windermere, was strangely comforting. After a while he left, and so I went back to my thoughts. The sun was higher, somewhere behind my legs as I swam. We were making progress.

In the February of 1986, finally, it snowed properly. There had been many days where snow 'settled', as Dad put it, but never like this. The days where it just settled before quickly melting always felt like a let-down; Father Christmas-like excitement where nightfall promised so much, only for things to return to normal in the morning, just with more aggravation and more traffic. The winter of 1986 had so far been dark, cold and grey, and with Christmas gone there was little promise of fun for months to come. Until this.

The secret radio hidden under my pillow confirmed it. Well after bedtime, with all the upstairs lights out, the disc jockey on LBC announced that London was being hit by a major snowstorm. As my favourite jingle played just before the 10 o'clock news I thought about the task ahead. There were at least three problems to solve: getting a day off school; persuading Mum that we had to go sledging; and finally, putting the never-used plastic sledges into action.

Flossie woke the house. She yelped and yapped at the back door knowing that something was new. I drew the bedroom curtains and gasped. Everything was pure white: the garden, the surrounding roofs, the trees in between. I ran down the stairs calling out excitedly to Mum and Dad as I passed their room. Anna appeared at her bedroom door wearing her dressing gown and a grin. I unlocked the back door. Flossie took a leap into the unknown, barking as she launched herself into the smooth whiteness piled up higher than the steps themselves. For a moment she disappeared beneath the surface, before carving herself a dog-sized hole and wriggling back to the top. The garden sounded different. It was so quiet – every little sound somehow muffled and muted. Better still, it was *still* snowing.

'School will be cancelled,' I announced confidently over an unusually formal family breakfast. Come to think of it, we never had breakfast together, so this was already a special day. Dad declared he would not give in to a 'bit of snow' and intended to drive to the office in Greenwich. In *his* day school would have 'gone ahead regardless'.

'Don't be so silly,' Mum replied. 'Besides, who on earth would come to see you today anyway?'

'I think we should all go to the park, together,' interjected Anna, pre-empting any paternal retaliation, '. . . with the sledges.' She paused again. '. . . And take *Flossie*,' she added with a satisfied look. 'She's very excited.' Her suggestion silenced the impromptu family conference, which was now effectively over.

Flossie was often a unifier when it came to family meetings, despite not being able to talk. It was an accepted fact that Anna was her chosen spokesperson. Many family arguments had been avoided in recent months by acquiescing to Flossie's unspoken wishes. I finished my Marmite toast and decided to take on the last of the three problems. The sledges were in the shed, and the shed was at the bottom of the snow-bound garden.

By the Friday after the Monday much of the snow had melted, but life still felt better for its visit. Dad only took one day off work, school was back on by Wednesday, and the sledging on the Tuesday had been far less fun – newly formed ice made it painful to fall off at speed on the hills of Eltham Park.

The snowball fights at school were quite violent. Each year groups of boys came out onto the playing field in force, sticking together as a tribe and launching lumps of the icy compacted snow at other tribes both bigger and smaller than themselves. It reminded me of the scenes on the TV news of football fans running at each other, throwing the newly installed seats from the stadium, and anything else in the vicinity. Last year had been the same, but it was the miners fighting with the police instead. Dad said the miners' strike was about a 'battle for control', and about jobs, but that the football fans were just mindless. But there were no police at school to keep order, let alone mounted police who seemed to sort out the football fans' and miners' fights, and so some of us came off the field with a bloody nose.

By Thursday the comedy willy on the big snowman on the playing field had fallen off, but the sludge and slush clung on regardless. The roads were moving again, the grey-black icy edging making everything look dirty. I was relieved. It meant there was no reason not to go to the baths on Friday after school, and to see John.

'Tefal, I want you to come to the hydropool after school on Fridays from now on,' John had announced at the end of the summer of 1985, following my first trip to the Lakes. 'I need some help with the youngsters.'

I was pleased to no longer be considered a youngster myself. After all, I was nearly nine, could swim at least a mile in the cold, do all four strokes well, and, unlike some of the older swimmers, do a full length of underwater breaststroke in the big pool with one breath. I even knew all the latest pop songs. And I had a nickname – Tefal. I had a big forehead, so when the company that made kettles, irons and other kitchen appliances put an advert on the telly featuring a nutty professor with an impossibly large forehead, I was named after that. I didn't mind the nickname, and was relieved to finally have one that stuck, though I was upset to learn from Dad that the company in question was French. The initial slapping of my forehead, known as 'spamming', was a pain, but this died down once people got bored of it. All in all, I felt I really belonged, and helping with youngsters made this true most of all.

The little hydrotherapy pool resembled a giant elevated bath tub, with a fence halfway across that separated the shallow and deep water. It was hot rather than warm, and full of chlorine, which made my eyes sting if I didn't wear goggles. The sessions were for toddlers and smaller children up to the age of five, and John needed me to keep an eye on the bigger children in the deeper part of the pool, while he coaxed and cajoled the smallest in the shallow part. I enjoyed messing around with the kids, watching them grow in confidence. Often the bigger ones would want to wrestle and be thrown around. After a few weeks, some of the parents began to thank me at the end of the session. Once the children could doggy-paddle and stay afloat, they were considered too good for the class and would leave. I wondered if any of them would join the swimming club in years to come.

Anna said it was considered a massive honour to be asked to help out at the hydropool. It proved I was becoming one of 'John's favourites'. I could see other evidence to support this. Once the pool was empty John and I would play around for a few minutes. As the weeks passed we developed a spoof slow-motion underwater wrestling routine, which started with some hand to hand combat and ended with me 'submitting' once trapped in a submerged head lock. John was strong. As we faced each other underwater before a bout he reminded me of one of those big oval-shaped contact mines from the war that could now be seen at the seaside in Broadstairs, painted red, and idly collecting money from passers-by. Submerged he hovered, weightless, controlling his buoyancy with the air in his lungs – poised to attack at the slightest approach. His goggled round face, set beneath his balding dented head, would adopt a mischievous toothy grin, like a Halloween pumpkin. He was half villain, half superhero. Upon provocation his wrestling moves would tie me in a knot in a split second. I fought back as hard as I could, but always lost in the end.

Our conversations were playful too. John was a hard man, but he also had a kinder, child-like aspect that I had latched onto. 'You want to watch out, John,' I said once we were upstairs in his office.

'Oh *reeeeally*?' he replied in his messing about voice, giggling as he did so. 'Why is that then, Young *Teeeeeefal*?'

'Because unless you're careful I'll have to duff you up,' I said. 'Show you who's boss,' I added, laughing at the cheek of it.

'It would take a *WHOLE ARMY* of Little Teeeefals to duff me up,' replied John with a half smile.

The exchange of threats soon became an extended part of the routine – one of those jokes that becomes funnier the more often it gets used. John was much less serious when it was just the two of us. He was hard to truly know, but I knew I liked him – he was exciting to be around, and I credited him with being responsible for all the swimming adventures of the previous few months, and for my new friends in the swimming club. I also wanted him to like me in return and felt good when he took an interest in me or teased me about something.

John sent me to the vending machines with some change for a toffee bar and a cup of hot chocolate. He said I had earned it because I helped out every week.

By the time I got back to the office Dad had arrived to collect me and was chatting amicably with John about nothing in particular. According to Anna, John had a reputation for being quite difficult with some parents, and because I liked him I hoped this would not apply to us. I had also begun to hope John and Dad would be friends, but in Dad's company John was very formal.

'Bye, John. See you tomorrow,' I called back as we left. I would be back at the pool in the morning. These days John let me go swimming for free on Saturday mornings, and provided I was there early and did a quick twenty lengths in the big pool before the public arrived, I could stay on for as long as I wanted. The lifeguards knew me too, so I was allowed to dive from the high boards, do somersaults from the poolside, and hold my breath at the bottom of the deep end for as long as possible without one of them diving in to rescue me.

Once spring came Mum and Dad decided to let me walk from the house to the pool on my own, provided I went down the High Street. On one occasion when Anna decided to come with me, John gave us £5 to share in the Wimpy on the way home. McDonald's was not allowed, but Wimpy was. Anna insisted we went to the Our Price record shop en route and bought herself a Pet Shop Boys album she had been saving for.

'How are you feeling?' asked John from under his bobble hat. He leaned on the rail in the same space JC had occupied and looked down at me as I trod water with both legs and one arm. The other arm was holding a chocolate digestive out of the sea as I munched on it. It had been held up by John as a signal to approach the boat and then lobbed overboard for me to catch just seconds earlier. I bobbed, chewed, and considered my response. Some hours had passed, but I didn't know how many. The thudding of the diesel engine was loud, and the fumes were unpleasant. I noticed the round exhaust hole at the stern, on the same side of the boat I was facing. I would have to swim further up from now on to avoid the fumes and prevent them making me sick.

'OK . . . fine,' I said with some confidence. The moment of speaking out loud to another person was itself a treat – a boost to morale. 'How are we doing?' I followed up. It was unusual for me to ask this of John (it somehow felt insubordinate) but the question betrayed my underlying anxiety.

'You're doing really well, Tefal. I want you to settle in for a couple of hours now. Cover off some of the distance.' He seemed upbeat, almost excited. There was little else to discuss. I wanted to continue the conversation, but couldn't think of anything to say.

'Can I have another biscuit?' I ventured, my mouth spluttering the crumbs of the first.

'No,' came the reply.

'OK. See you in a couple of hours then,' I said matter-of-factly, before resuming my stroke and drifting back off into my private world.

1986 was one of those years when big things just kept on happening – the snow was merely the start. There was even a football World Cup in Mexico. That meant not only two sticker albums to complete in the same season, but also that Gary Lineker and Peter Shilton, my favourite players (apart from Leyton Orient's Alan Comfort and Peter 'Bomber' Wells), were on the telly more. Orient were never on the telly. Dad, meanwhile, was obsessed by the news, and so was Dr Lynsky, my new form tutor, so there was no getting away from other global events.

When the Space Shuttle *Challenger* exploded we all talked about it in the playground seriously like grown-ups, though a joke was doing the rounds by the end of the day. When the nuclear reactor exploded at Chernobyl one boy in the year below was made to wear a dust mask to school by his mum, so we teased him mercilessly until he took it off. And when the AIDS advert came out on TV Roger Rat-Bag said it was dangerous to have sex with an iceberg. I sort of got it, so I told Dad, who said it was very funny. I was now old enough to stay up for the 9 o'clock news, which made a few things – mostly the politics, which Dad loved to talk about – slot into place, but other things, like girls, maths and how to beat Anna at anything, were still a mystery. Happily, Anna took the train to school on her own, so I got to ask Dad the most important of life's questions for fifteen minutes every day on the way to school in the car:

'Dad. Why can't we go on holiday on a plane? To Spain, like Rog. Or Florida, like Ellis? Why do we have to go on a canal boat all the time?'

Something about money and 'interest rates' (whatever they were) confirmed the answer was no.

'Can we have Capital on instead of Radio 4? Anna says it's the best radio station.'

A straight 'No'.

'Can I go to the disco at school next Friday?'

'Erm, yes, but I believe you're helping John at the hydropool? You ought to check with him.'

Meanwhile, the fast lane on a Wednesday night was hard work. After last summer's Windermere trip Anna and I were in the top group. The Senior swimmers were still much faster than me, but the swim sets were the same for everyone. After a long set, like twenty lengths of crawl or a 4x4 medley, I was breathing so hard that my head felt dizzy and I couldn't quite see properly. The chemicals in the pool made things worse; everything – the air I gulped, and the water itself – felt mildly toxic compared to the open water. Once home I put cold cucumber slices on my eyes to relieve the soreness. The hardest bit was getting out at the end of each set, joining the back of the queue and starting all over again. Just concentrating on what was to be done next was challenging. Often I fell so far behind that the next set had already started by the time I got out. If I missed John's instructions from the poolside, which only ever came once, I just had to dive straight back in again and copy what was happening in front of me.

After training I went to John's office. I would always say hello and goodbye to him as I came and went. My trips to Eltham Baths had become more frequent: Wednesdays for club night; Friday for hydropool duties or a late evening training session; Saturdays when I would train on my own before having free time; and Sundays when I would train with the Senior group or do demonstration drills for John's life-saving class, which was open to the public. I knew everyone at the pool, and they knew me – the lifeguards, Beryl the kiosk lady (who always admitted me for free), and John himself, who was always there. The baths had become a safe and familiar place, like home, or even school, where I had also begun to discover more confidence. That night, a couple of parents were walking out of John's office as I approached, shaking their heads and rolling their eyes. 'He's so bloody difficult!' muttered one to the other. Unbowed, I burst in.

'John, can I go to a disco on Friday instead of the hydropool, please?'

John sighed, without looking up from behind his desk. 'Why do you want to do that, Tefal?' he eventually replied.

'Because Roger Rat-Bag and Quilts are going, and because there will be girls there . . . from Anna's school.'

'So this is a *Colfe's* disco then, eh?' John enquired, looking up suddenly, although he already knew this given it was where I went to school. 'Colfe's is a school for wankers.' He looked back down as he said it.

I didn't reply. John had begun to say this to tease me lately and usually I took no notice. Everyone was teased about something, often something visually obvious. In my case my forehead and school were the main sources of ammunition. However, on this occasion it seemed to matter. Still I said nothing. There was a long, awkward pause.

'Who are "Rat-Bag" and "Quills" anyway?' asked John in a derisory tone.

'It's Quilts, not Quills. They're my best friends . . . at school anyway,' I added, sensing his unease at the possibility that anything, or anyone, could be more important to me than swimming and the club.

Another pause.

'OK. You can go. But I want to meet this *Rat-Bag* . . . He sounds like trouble.'

I thanked him as I ran out the door to find Anna and Dad. John shouted after me from the office. 'TEFAL!' he bellowed, so I stopped on demand and looked back.

'Better make it 7 a.m. on Saturday then . . . and thirty lengths before free time.'

'OK, John,' I called over my shoulder, grinning as I resumed my exit plan.

'. . . And bring RAT-BAG!' I heard, just, as I passed the ticket kiosk. I had made a good deal.

I asked Mum what I should wear to the disco. I had been to a swimming club disco so I knew broadly what to expect, but a school disco might be a different proposition. I wondered if there would be a raffle. I had only ever entered one raffle, but having won a clock radio, which was now in my room and a prized possession, I was keen to enter another.

There would be two years of boys and two years of girls. Mum said that if girls were going it was best to be smart; girls liked boys who were smart. My smartest outfit had been purchased for a recent family occasion. It consisted of grey flannel trousers, a white shirt with a 'wing collar' and a very smart clip-on red bowtie. 'Shall I wear my bowtie then, Mum?' I said.

'Yes, good idea. I'll iron your special shirt.'

On the way there, Rat-Bag's mum, who I liked very much, complimented me on my bowtie, as if to prove Mum's point. Roger, however, who was wearing much cooler clothes, surveyed me in silence across the back seat as I fastened my seatbelt. His silence suggested some unease at my turnout.

The main school hall felt sparsely populated, the space too large for the size of the group. Clusters of boys and girls stood, segregated, against the walls, too scared to venture into what had become a dancefloor in the middle. The DJ on stage boomed familiar pop songs through enormous black speakers – a gantry of flashing lights above his head, and, just like on *Top of the Pops*, a smoke machine occasionally emitted clouds of mysterious vapour. Eventually we began to dance in circular groups. After half an hour or so I plucked up the courage to ask one of the Blackheath girls to dance. I was not very good at dancing, unlike Rog who was confidently displaying a range of moves, most of which reminded me of a robot. My dancing was more of a side-to-side wobble despite having picked up some tips at the swimming club discos. Neither my dance partner nor I looked at each other as we wobbled. I was in time, she was not. I soon regretted having asked her at all. At the end of the song I was relieved to get a tap on the shoulder from Roger. He beckoned me outside to where Adam Mawyer, the tallest boy in the year, was waiting. They stood shoulder to shoulder and I knew something was wrong, although Roger was too nice to look intimidating. 'Greg. Me and Rat-Bag think you are moving in on our birds,' said Mawyer.

'No I'm not!' I protested, upset at the accusation and being ganged up on.

'Yeah, you are,' said Roger, 'and you're wearing a bowtie – making us look bad.' His words caused a pain inside me.

'So you better back off our birds, Greg! Got it?' said Mawyer aggressively, jabbing his finger in my direction. They walked back into the hall, leaving me standing.

I ran out into the car park and started to cry. It didn't stop. Half an hour later Dad arrived to pick me up. I told him the whole sorry episode, struggling to blurt it out. He seemed to understand, but, in a way that often happened with Dad, things sounded like they would get worse before they got better.

'That's not the last time you will cry over a girl, Tom, believe me. Just wait until you get older!

. . . Don't worry, son,' Dad continued. 'Just think, you'll be back in the pool first thing tomorrow.

. . . And besides, I reckon young Mawyer put Rog up to it anyway. Rog is your best friend.' I stopped crying at that remark, but still fell short of a reply.

'. . . I'm sure John would agree with me . . . for what it's worth . . .' he tailed off. I considered the point. John would agree. Maybe I should have gone to the hydropool after all. I decided to invite Roger to come swimming next Saturday to meet John, as requested, provided we were still best friends.

We drove home. 'You've changed the radio!' I said in surprise, snapping out of my misery. It was playing 'Saving All My Love for You' by Whitney Houston, who had gone straight to number one. The same song had made the tears harder to control just moments earlier as it echoed from the school hall while I waited in the car park for Dad to transport me home.

'Have I? Oh yes, maybe I did . . . I quite like this one.'

Dad and I went for a long walk through London along the Regent's Canal that Sunday. Unlike most people I knew, Dad thought all canals were interesting, especially when they passed through cities. I took my Walkman in the expectation that things might get just too boring, but Dad and I chatted frequently in between moments of comfortable silence. We walked under the Thames through the foot tunnel to the docks, and then to Limehouse where we picked up the towpath through the East End. Much of this part of London was now a building site, punctuated by hidden communities. The canal was full of debris, and the sky was full of rain.

'Dad, do you think I should swim the Channel one day?' I asked as we strode past a park in Hackney.

'Well, that really depends.' He paused. 'Do you want to?'

'Maybe,' I offered.

Dad paused again.

'What made you ask me that, why now?'

'Not sure really. But I've been thinking about it a lot.'

'Well, that's understandable,' he said. 'It looks to me as if John may have the same idea. It would explain all the things he's asking you to do.'

Anna and I were now part of the core group of swimmers, but John had recently started to single me out to do more and more swimming. I found that I wanted to be around him – to follow him. Everything that happened at the club came with a sense of fun and adventure, which often revolved around John himself. The notice board of the baths flashed into my mind. I realized I wanted to be on it – somehow.

'But *could* I, Dad? Do you think I could do it one day?'

'Of course,' he said without hesitation. 'You of all people could do anything if you really wanted to, Tom. No doubt about that at all.'

We went back to companionable silence and walked in step, winding our way along the towpath, heading further west towards Camden Lock. A man with shabby shoes and a straggly beard shivered inside a blanket under a bridge, sheltering from the rain. Another man, holding a beer can, wobbled towards us. The graffiti all around us gave the place a threatening feel – as if we were trespassing. Dad shook his head as we passed an open lock gate, and we pushed it shut to prevent any more water being lost. Gradually the urban decay gave way to smarter surroundings. The colours of Camden Market appeared on one side, and the smell of frying onions made me hungry. It was a smell I recognized from the terraces at Orient, where Dad and I now watched football every other Saturday afternoon after swimming.

Anna's favourite Pet Shop Boys track, 'West End Girls', played over and over in my head – the music in time with our steps. The song was made for London, and the moment on the towpath with Dad. I strode out, to keep pace.

As the summer of 1986 approached, the news was full of stories about radioactive sheep in the Lake District after Chernobyl, and the risks to tourists. Palfrey's grandfather refused to let him come to Windermere because of it. Mum and Dad didn't seem to mind as Anna and I were back there again. The camp began in the same way, but I was not homesick this time. There was no storm either, so we went for a swim in the stream. It glided quickly and deeply through the campsite, running clear and promising adventure. I wore my goggles and floated along the surface in the flow on my own for a while, studying the underwater world.

A fish! A large fish, larger than any I had seen before, lurked behind a submerged rock in midstream. He (if it was a he) must have seen me as I floated past on the current a few feet above him. He was elegant and required barely any movement of his body to hold station. He faced upstream, in the lesser flow of water that was eddying invisibly in the lee of the rock. His olive-green back was freckled with small dark dots. His beady eyes looked straight ahead.

I knew that all animals were of a type, a breed, like Flossie who was a mongrel according to Dad, but a 'cross-breed' according to Anna. I wondered what type of fish he was. Probably just a 'large spotty' one. With my stronger right arm I turned myself into the flow and kicked down towards him, arms out in front. He was away in a flash, upstream through the current. I gave chase, swimming hard against the flow, but lost sight of him quickly. I wondered how he could get so far upstream, and so far uphill from the lake. Why would he want to? Windermere was the nicest place to swim in the world; no chlorine, and with more space than any fish or boy could need. As I floated and swam, I realized that I was back in a place that I loved.

The rasping sound of the outer-tent zip being pulled slowly upwards broke the dawn silence. Nothing else sounded like it. It roused me from my half sleep and I glanced slowly and nervously around the boys' tent. John's sleeping bag was empty. It lay on the other side of another vacant sleeping bag, which belonged to Tetley. Then there was me. I was no longer at the end of the line. In fact, I slept just two places along from John, which, a promotion of sorts, brought its own sense of achievement. John was yet to enter the inner tent to select his target. I lay flat to avoid attention. I was nine and three-quarters and, despite all the improvements to my swimming in the last year, I had no desire at all to be sent on a solo attempt in the lake.

There were two entrances to the inner tent. The one furthest away from me was gently unzipped – a different sound, like a buzzing fly on account of the smaller zip. In his sharp stage whisper John ordered Bear to get up. There was no response and so John's chubby hand appeared through the gap and tugged hard at the foot of Bear's sleeping bag.

'Bear! Fuckin' get up.' Bear groaned. I exhaled as the knot in my stomach began to untie itself, the tension becoming unbridled relief. As Bear slid out to get himself changed, the heads of my fellow sleepers began to rise up, one by one, grinning in silence at one another. I had not been the only one awake after all.

It was a beautiful day. Our swimming spot at Belle Isle was bathed in hot sunshine and towels were laid on the grass for us to sunbathe between swims. Anna had done this year's mix tape, which played a happy sequence of songs.

Giant and I (Lee was his real name, but he was short for his age) were searching the CB channels, calling out onto the airwaves to start a conversation with yet undiscovered fellow enthusiasts. I had decided my handle was Top Cat, in homage to my favourite cartoon character. Giant stuck with Giant, but prefaced it with 'The' to impart gravitas. Sound thinking, given that anyone who replied was unlikely to meet him in the flesh.

Dennis and Cynthia sat in deckchairs under a nearby sycamore tree on the shoreline. Dennis had his transistor radio with him; partly to escape the barrage of a ninety minute repeating cycle of pop music, and partly because there was a Royal Wedding on. Prince Andrew was marrying Sarah Ferguson. People seemed less fussed about this wedding compared to his older brother's. 'It won't last,' Cynthia observed from under her tree.

There was no answer on the CB, so Giant and I went to the water's edge to throw stones. We sat around the bus, ate hot soup from the portable stove, and made jam sandwiches on the fat white bread. We waited for Bear's arrival at the halfway rendezvous. We would swim out and see him on the tiny island in the normal way.

The boat came ashore before we had a chance to react, but not at the island rendezvous. John had been calling on the CB but Giant and I had left it on the wrong channel, so the call went unheard. It was rowed in hard on two sets of oars, directly in front of where the bus was parked on the shore. Bear, wrapped up in layers of heavy clothing, had swum well but was pulled out at the 4.5 mile point with cramp. John and Tetley had rowed him quickly to Belle Isle, probably just over a mile further north. He wasn't cold and looked cheery enough. I felt sorry for him that the swim was abandoned as I now knew that cramp could often just be a case of bad luck.

'Tefal,' ordered John from the boat, 'get your kit on.'

I felt nauseous. This was it. I looked around at the others, hoping for support. The faces looked back in sympathy. Anna gave me an encouraging smile. I walked off from the group to be on my own. Perhaps John knew it was me who'd left the CB on the wrong channel and this was my punishment. I half hid behind a tree to change into my wet trunks, and tried to process what was happening. John had probably decided that I was to swim the northern section, some 4.5 miles to Ambleside. My first proper solo attempt had arrived, yet nothing else was said – no instructions, no 'good luck', or hint that there was even a choice to be made. A minute or two later I stood nervously in the shallows, shaking my arms, waiting. New supplies were loaded onto the boat as I adjusted my goggles. 'OK, Tefal. When you're ready!' shouted John, now afloat some 20 metres offshore.

I walked in as I always did, with purpose, my heart racing. Just before the depth where I normally launched forwards and dived into deeper water, I glanced back and paused. The group were standing in a tight huddle now, looking on with a collective air of concern. Breaking the silence they began to call out words of encouragement, and so changed the mood . . . 'Go, Tefal!' 'You can do it, Tefal!' 'See you in Ambleside, Tefal!' There had been no time to fully process the challenge that lay ahead, but as my friends cheered and waved my heart filled with something that felt like courage and so I dived for the boat in front of me. My best, fastest front crawl, powered by a surge of adrenaline, meant I was upon it within a few strokes. The boat turned gently northwards, towards the large, mountain-lined expanse of the lake that lay beyond Belle Isle, and I turned with it. Tetley, bare-chested and wearing sunglasses, was on the oars, dabbing them rhythmically to achieve a pace I could manage. The blue and white flags were raised. John sat on the back bench under the blue and white bobble hat, despite the sunshine. He studied me, and in the brief moment where I could see him on each breath I took, I studied him back. We were away.

They had to haul me into the rowing boat without it tipping over. The boat was already unstable and at least a mile off Ambleside, in the widest, wildest part of the lake. A summer wind had blown in, accelerating through the mountains, funnelling its way through the Langdale valley, and Lake Windermere had become an entirely different place. For the first time as far as swimming was concerned, I was scared. During the momentary eye contact I had with the crew I looked for a sign of understanding as the conditions began to overwhelm me. The choppy waves were becoming too hard to swim through. My arms were hitting water when they should have been reaching forwards through the air. My stomach was full from gulping in mouthfuls of the lake when trying to breathe; I wondered if it made me less buoyant. I spluttered every few strokes and my shoulders and legs were hurting; aching from the repetition of front crawl. I was also cold, colder than I could remember. Crying into my goggles, I stopped. I tried to tell John that I couldn't carry on. My numb lips struggled to form words. I could see my hands jolting and shaking. All the muscles in my body felt taut. I was in a slow-motion freezing state of panic. Aged nine, I was in the process of failing something, other than a maths test, for the first time: the 4.5 mile swim to Ambleside.

'What's the matter, Tefal?' asked John after a few minutes of my being on the boat. No words had been shared up until this point. Shivering violently, I had been helped into some clothes by Tetley and narrowly avoided falling back into the lake as the boat rocked with our movements. John stayed on the oars, pulling the boat through the wind and waves while Tetley helped me get dry. I was confused, and felt very tired, but I was no longer out of breath. A woolly hat appeared from the plastic box and was placed on my head. Tetley, true to his name, filled a plastic cup with warm sweet tea from a flask. I drank it slowly, hands shaking, and looked around the vast lake that surrounded us. The mile-wide gap between the eastern and western shores was gently narrowing and in front I could make out the masts of moored crafts, and roofs of Ambleside, set against the backdrop of the highest mountains further north. I realized there had probably been only another mile or two to go.

A chocolate digestive came next. Then another. I drank and ate in silence, but the strong wind made enough noise for all three of us. The sun came out, warming me through the layers that now covered my body. The glistening lake was wild and beautiful and we were deep within her middle. Waves were still slapping the underside of the boat's hull, as if trying to push us directly back in protest. From the safety of the rowing boat, they looked smaller and far less hostile. I began to feel embarrassed, as if I had made a fuss over nothing. I struggled to understand the contrast between what I had been going through and how things seemed from up here. All right for them, I thought, resenting how little empathy John and Tetley were showing, you try swimming in that lot. Tetley made his way, awkwardly, past John to the oars on the forward rowing bench to add more speed to our journey to shore, leaving me alone on the aft bench facing John, with no means of escape or diversion. John repeated the question:

'I said, what's the matter, Tefal?' and this time I had to think of a reply.

'I think . . . I think the wind made me try and swim faster . . . because I was trying to fight through the waves.'

'And?' he probed.

'And because I was swimming faster, I got tired quicker.' Things started to make sense as I said them out loud. 'And you always say that once you're tired, the cold is harder to take. So I got cold.'

John pulled the oars and recovered them in a smooth motion. His chubby hands needed no instructions from his brain to do this. He auto-repeated the stroke. I noticed his face had become burned, his skin and lips chapped by the sun, wind and rain. No wonder he wore a bobble hat over his thinning pate. His expression was even, not angry. As if trying to solve a puzzle, he gazed out onto the lake, and took his time replying.

'Sounds about right,' he eventually said, calmly. 'But what about all that fuckin' sulking in the water then? What was all that about?'

'What sulking?' I said defensively, unaware that I had communicated my feelings at all while actually swimming.

'I *saw* you, *Teeeefal*,' he said, in the gently mocking tone I recognized from times we spent alone.

'. . . Bottom lip, tears, talking to yourself underwater and messing up your breathing . . .' He could have gone on, I realized.

'I think I got a bit scared.'

'Scared of what, exactly?'

'I'm . . . well, I'm not exactly sure now,' I said honestly. John seized his moment.

'Poor little *Teeeeefal*, boo hoo hoo!' he teased, as if on stage in a pantomime. He would have pretended to rub his eyes with his fists like a baby had he not been rowing. Tetley joined in from the front of the boat. John continued, 'Boo hoo, Teefal, *scared* of the water,' baiting me for a reaction. His smiling face portrayed mockery rather than spite and my initial anger at the humiliation was replaced by an unexpected feeling: I wanted to laugh – at myself. This annoyed me as I desperately didn't want to give in to the teasing. It was the same trick I used on Anna all the time, I realized. I gradually broke into a smile I couldn't control and chuckled back at them both. The tension was gone, carried away on the wind towards the fells. Perhaps I had been scared of failing John, rather than the swim, and of being in trouble. Perhaps it was possible to simply laugh in the face of failure, and move on.

'Can you row, Tefal?' asked John after the moment had died.

'Sort of. I tried it last year but didn't get very far.'

'Well, you need to be able to row if you want to crew a swim boat, with me.' The last two words meant the most. 'Tetley, take over, and teach Tefal to row. I'm having a nap.'

Moments later I was sitting on the main oars bench, feeling important. John was behind me, lying down in the prow of the boat, snuggled around a few bags of kit, bobble hat over his eyes, asleep. Tetley was now on the aft bench, instructing me on how best to row against the wind, which had strengthened again as we headed north. Eventually I got the hang of it and so Tetley sat back, content to let me do things with no direction. I could not be sure, given he was wearing mirrored dog-eared sunglasses, but the motion of his head suggested that he too was falling asleep. It was my job to get us safely to shore now.

The wind was determined and relentless. Blisters started to form on the palms of my water-softened hands but I didn't mind. A large sailing boat came past the stern, leaning heavily over on its side, with just the smallest of sails hoisted on the mast to deflect the wind. I marvelled at its speed and the fact that, unlike speed-boats, it made no noise to go so fast. It looked likely to tip over and capsize at any moment. Two crew members sat on the top rail to help balance the boat and maybe prevent this. They waved at me, and although I couldn't wave back because I was holding the oars, I nodded vigorously in acknowledgement. I felt like we were in the same small club of people who understood something. These elements, this place, and Lake Windermere, were hard to tame even when the sun was out. But if I couldn't swim it, clearly I had to row it instead.

The following day the outer zip made the familiar unzipping noise. No one moved. Quiet footsteps padded over to the right-hand entrance to the inner tent, which meant that either me or Tetley, who had done two straight days on the boat, were going for a long swim. I sat up in my sleeping bag. Giant, who remained motionless, looked up at me with 'are you mad?' eyes. I unzipped the inner tent myself to see John's shoes, and so I poked my head out and looked up at him. He smiled, nodded, and walked out of the tent in silence. Five minutes later I was in the food tent eating porridge. An hour later we were on the water's edge at Ambleside. Two and a half hours after that I had completed my first long distance open water swim, having covered nearly 5 miles to Belle Isle. I was by far the youngest swimmer on the camp, so I knew this might be quite a big deal. That night, for the first time, I sat in one of the two chairs reserved for swimmers, although I had long since recovered. The last mile was the hardest thing I could remember in my lifetime, but the fear of the previous day's attempt had gone, along with the aggressive wind that fuelled it. Conditions mattered, and today, though grey and full of drizzle, had been benign in swimming terms. John took the oars himself to row me in, which was itself a form of encouragement. Above all, I realized I desperately wanted to get there myself.

Making the distance felt better than Orient winning 3–0 at home. In fact, it surpassed everything I could think of, even completing a sticker album. As I drifted off to sleep that night I realized something else. It was much better to make the distance, no matter how unpleasant the journey.

This year, while wandering Bowness with Anna after the one-mile width event at the end of the week, I used my remaining money for just one souvenir: a navigation chart of Windermere that I had seen displayed on the Pier heads where the ferries came and went. It came rolled up, because it was very long from top to bottom and the width of a newspaper from side to side. It showed all the markers I now recognized – headlands, islands, shore marks and surrounding peaks. I studied it for hours in the months that followed; if I ever got to make an attempt of the full length of Windermere, I wanted to know where I was. And in the months before I was here again, I could remember the place, and my friends, just by looking at the map.

The rest of the summer seemed to last a very long time. Anna and I were old enough to do things on our own, so we did. John had arranged for us to have free access to the open air lido in Eltham Park. It was a beautiful old place. There were wooden cubicles on both sides and at one end was a turnstile-guarded entrance house, which also housed a basket system where we handed in our clothes in exchange for a big rubber band with a number on it. At the other end a broken fountain sat at the top of some concrete steps, with lots of space to roll out towels and lie in the sun. What we liked best was the small kiosk that sold tea, chocolate bars and penny sweets. We went to the lido every day, almost without fail, and even when it rained, but on a hot summer's day, in fact on any day, the clean cold water was the best thing to swim in by far. The only mystery was why we had the place almost completely to ourselves.

Most *new* swimming pools came with giant plastic slides and wave machines, and were shaped in a way that made proper swimming impossible. They were also located miles away from anywhere because they needed more space. Even the big pool at Eltham was to have a large flume fitted in an attempt to keep up with the competition. Dad said that lidos were no longer fashionable, and that he feared ours would also close one day. Apparently, lidos had been very popular in the old days but, like most old things, they were neglected now, in a state of disrepair and generally undervalued.

The endless summer days melted into one another. Anna and I began to feel protective about the lido, which we considered our own. We could last a whole day on 50 pence between us since, thanks to John's standing orders to the pool staff, we didn't have to pay to get in. I would buy strawberry shoelaces and cola bottle penny sweets with my share. Anna liked Wham fizzy chew bars. Often we were joined by others. Cousin Vicky would let our phone ring twice to notify us that she'd be round in five minutes to walk to the lido. Sometimes Palfrey would come and I wondered if he had any brothers or sisters of his own because he seemed to like the company of Anna and me. Best of all, on some summer evenings, and having already spent the whole day swimming, I would go back to the lido with Dad once he got home from work. His shirt would be soaked in sweat from a hot drive through the rush hour. His face was sometimes anxious and weary, and I loved seeing it change to one of joy once he sploshed messily into the deep end and the cold water rushed his senses. He looked funny in his old faded trunks – his big hairy body reminded me of a cartoon bear. Dad knew how to swim – a slow and very deliberate style – but that summer I realized that I had become better at something than my father. These were easily the happiest days on record. I had to think about exactly what day of the week it was because they all felt the same. But it couldn't last forever.

The coming school year was increasingly on my mind as that perfect summer drew to a close. I had Common Entrance exams to sit in January, and I would have to pass Grade Three on my cello if I wanted to join the school orchestra. Music was a very big deal at school and, with the exception of winding up Anna and going to see Orient, had become my main interest outside of swimming. But as the summer holiday came to an end, something even more important happened. With the Channel swim season now in full swing and the water temperature at its warmest, Anna, now twelve, was selected by John as the youngest member of that year's Channel relay team. I wasn't the only person in the family who had learned to swim properly.

I made up my mind to swim the Channel at a club Christmas gathering for the Channel Swimming team that winter. The party ran late into the night in a small house belonging to the Vine family on the estate behind Eltham Baths. Anna was surrounded by her five successful cross-Channel team mates, who took turns recounting tales of the crossing to France: the cold sea, the dark hours, the unity and the laughter, the fatigue. According to Mum, that swim represented the biggest achievement in our family since I was born. I sat with the older swimmers wishing I was part of their team, part of Anna's team.

John sent for me from the kitchen. I felt a rush of excitement and apprehension; what might he want with me? I had begun to crave his company and wanted to spend time with him one-to-one. John spoke and I obeyed – as did everyone else. I reported to the kitchen, to find him with a glass of brandy in hand, surrounded by an entourage of club stalwarts.

This was John's world – former club swimmers, trusted connections from the Channel Swimming community, and a few parents who had shared the journey of the club he had now built into a group of nearly a hundred youngsters from the local area. He had no family of his own, Anna claimed – in fact, it was hard to get any information about John at all, especially from him. On the few occasions I had asked him anything about himself, such as where he was from, he would always find a diversion, or simply reply with 'Never you mind, Young Tefal,' which left a sense of enduring mystery. Just last week Anna had shown me a press cutting of John being honoured for services to life saving – but for some reason it was not on the board at the pool.

An animated conversation continued in the small crowded kitchen as I approached, nervously. John was smiling, relaxed but in command. I waited for him to notice me as I looked up at this grown-up club. Ignored, I turned instead to the tray of food that sat on a folded half-table and eyed up some cubes of cheese. They were skewered by cocktail sticks and, sadly, combined with chunks of pineapple that would have to be removed without causing offence.

'. . . and I'm telling you, Dennis, it's not fuckin' 'appening,' demanded John, 'No kid has *ever* left my swimming club and signed on the dole. Never. And it ain't about to start either.' It was a well-known fact that many of the lifeguards in the borough were former club swimmers. Dad often talked about unemployment, and as an issue of the time it was visible everywhere – from the news, the Job Centre on the High Street, even the lyrics of Anna's favourite Wham! song.

'. . . right, Marcus?' added John, turning to face the man who stood by his side. I gasped.

Next to John was a tall, good-looking young man. He was overtly cool, with American-style clothes that included a baseball jacket, a faded t-shirt, pale blue jeans and Converse shoes. His expensive-looking watch caught what dim light was available and glistened. The man seemed comfortable despite the fact that he was on some level a stranger in this company. He stood next to John, shoulder to shoulder, and watched the room, smiling politely at the jokes and opinions that flew between the other adults, all of whom clutched cans of lager or glasses of brandy.

'Tefal!' blurted out John in surprise, as if happy to have located a lost item. I turned to face him, concealing a mouth full of cheddar, and hiding the sticks and pineapple chunks deftly behind my back. The adults parted slightly in a way that made John and the man standing next to him seem even more important.

'Tefal, I want you to meet someone.'

I nodded obediently, unwilling to reveal a mouthful of food by saying anything.

'Tefal, this is Marcus Hooper. I believe you know who he is?'

My eyes widened and so did my mouth, revealing my store of half-chewed cheese. Marcus Hooper, holder of the world record for the youngest person to swim the Channel, and probably the best swimmer in the club's history, held out his hand to shake mine, but I could only offer him a fistful of soggy pineapple and cocktail sticks in return so I began to stuff them into the pockets of my jeans.

'Tefal, *what* are you doing?' demanded John, shaking his

head in disbelief. 'This is *Marcus Hooper*!' he added in frustration before I finally swallowed the cheese.

'I know . . . Sorry, John.' I wiped the pineapple juice on my jeans and held out my somewhat sticky hand. Marcus was a legend; I had studied the notice board in the foyer of the pool forensically over the previous year, reading all the articles on his swim and admiring the photos. I had marvelled at the fact British Airways sent him on Concorde to mark the achievement.

'Hello, Marcus. You look very different to your photos,' I said nervously, hoping to divert attention from my clumsiness.

'Very nice to meet you, Tefal. Yes, I suppose I do these days,' he said, smiling back.

Marcus looked nothing like the black and white photos of him as a boy. They showed him in his trunks on the shore of the Channel, greased up and making 'V for Victory' signs with both hands, which somehow dated the image to an even earlier era. He had been very chubby, if not fat, standing on that beach years ago. But as a grown man, he was tall, handsome and slim. He was now seven years older than he had been the day he broke the world record aged twelve – a record that no one had been able to beat and that kept him in the *Guinness Book of Records* year on year since 1979.

'John has told me all about you,' he said.

'Don't bloody tell him that,' interjected John, 'he's got a big enough head already!'

Marcus ignored him. 'How's the training going?'

'OK, I think,' I answered, starstruck, glancing at John for some kind of reassurance. 'What do you do now? Are you still a swimmer?' I asked.

'Sort of. Well, no, not really. I work in the City.'

I knew that people who worked in the City were often in the news. They wore red braces, drove Porsche 911s, and some even had portable telephones. Most recently, they had apparently suffered the collective misfortune of a 'Big Bang', which, despite sounding extremely dangerous, had by all accounts come out rather well. People from the City were known mostly for making huge amounts of money and living a fast life. Indeed, if someone at school was well off, the chances were their dad worked in the City.

'Are you a Yuppie?' I asked, recalling that the youngest and wealthiest of the City cohort had acquired a new collective noun.

'Erm . . . I'm not sure really,' replied Marcus. 'I don't have a mobile phone, so no, probably not.' He smiled. I knew in that moment that not only did I like Marcus – even without a mobile phone he probably still drove a Porsche – but that he was my hero. So I made up my mind, in that exact moment of Christmas 1986, that I wanted to break his world record. I had recently turned ten, so if that was to happen before I was twelve, then the summer after next, 1988, would be the only time window when this was possible.

4. *Windermere*

10.15 a.m., 6 September 1988 – 5 hours, 14 miles off the French coast, English Channel

'How are you feeling?' came the question some time later, same as before. Time had passed. I did not know how much. The signal to approach the boat was new: John held up a fat stubby glass bottle. It looked like a Schweppes tonic bottle from the shape. The sort Dad would have in his drinks cabinet, maybe for ginger ale. John waved it gently from side to side until I noticed, and reacted. I had not done this before but the plan was obvious. He reached down precariously over the side of the boat as I approached, holding the bottle in one hand and the rail with the other. I swam gently towards him and held out an arm, with open hand in front of me. Both of us moved up and down with the sea so it took some thought. His grip on the bottle was by his fingertips, just on the neck. We had to avoid physical contact with one another at all costs. There was a fat, hand-sized glass body for me to grab, and so I grabbed it. It reminded me of the air-to-air refuelling process for war planes I had seen on the TV, where the nozzle and probe finally connect. Instantly I felt the warmth of the liquid through the glass in the palm of my hand. No mistaking the deep red content. My fuel was soup. Heinz tomato soup.

'Not too bad,' I said in reply. I had been in the water for some time now, maybe five hours, and my body knew it. My shoulder muscles were beginning to ache. My legs, at the join with the hip, the bit that always hurt on a long swim, were sore. My mind had wandered off into many different corners in the time since our last encounter. Suddenly I couldn't recall what I had been thinking about. Time had vanished.

It took me a moment to come round. It can become hard to really feel the surface world when swimming for a long time. The motions of the body and the water itself combine to shut off other senses; the relentless noise of the splashing around the ears, the constant turning of the head, rolling of the body and the oscillating view of light and dark cast their own spell. You have to stop swimming to notice how things really are. I held the bottle out of the water and swigged. 'Slowly, Tefal,' I thought I heard from a voice other than John's. The conditions seemed benign; the water was pretty flat – rolling rather than choppy. There was swell, and occasional big waves from the passing tankers and ferries somewhere in the vicinity, but things were calm. I had swum through much worse in the lake and on the coast. The sun was out. In fact, there was not a cloud in the sky. The lack of chop suggested barely any wind. It was hard to imagine better conditions.

The sweetness of the soup was sublime. My mouth had become accustomed to the saline flavours of the sea, but my tongue had already started to protest and was swollen. The boat and I moved up and down on the swell as if on opposite ends of a see-saw, while I savoured the taste and the warmth running through me. My faculties began to return.

'How are we doing?' I asked back. John and I had found our own drill of question and answer already. We were good at this.

'Really well, Tefal.' He took a deep breath before he continued. He looked away from me to prepare himself, then looked back. 'You are halfway,' he went on, forcing a smile.

Halfway. Two bewildering emotions arrived immediately and were at once in conflict. The first was panic. I already felt like I had given my best and swum further, and probably faster, than I had ever swum before. Only halfway. Crushing. How would I ever finish? This had to be impossible.

I looked over my left shoulder with the intent of harnessing the other thought. If we were halfway then I should be able to see . . .

There it was. A clear thin white line was just visible where the grey-brown water met the blue sky. There were black smudges on the line too. England . . . and then the second emotion; hope.

John was reading my thoughts. He would know how this would feel, and that it was crucial to manage my reaction.

'Tefal, listen to me, lad.' He leaned over the rail once more and extended his hand in a chopping motion to stress the point he wanted to make. 'We are five hours in. Just five hours,' he emphasized. 'And we are halfway. You are on for a sub ten hour swim here.' With those words, part of me wanted to cry, but confusingly the other part felt an early sense of euphoria. If John thought I could do it, clearly implied with 'sub ten hours', then it was true. I just had to swim the other half. At ten hours it would be two and a half hours more than my longest ever swim, but so what? 'Over halfway already!' I said to myself.

I clung onto the soup in its fat stubby bottle and took another swig. I would need all of it, so I kept swigging. I looked up again, in search of England. I had to confirm I had actually seen what I thought I had seen. This time the light had changed – the sun was now gleaming off the white cliffs. Perhaps there had been some broken cloud on the coastline masking the brightness of the reflected light. The thin dark smudges either side came into focus; the shoreline of Kent ran away on either side of the cliffs, before disappearing and becoming sky again. I looked over my right shoulder. France was no longer visible. I kept looking to confirm this. On the rise of the swell, I just saw a faint dark mark on the horizon. I had left France well and truly behind. I just had to swim home.

Just six months after meeting Marcus Hooper at the Christmas party, and after some punishing sessions in the pool, John decided it was time for me to attempt Windermere on my own, aged ten. The two events were linked; little by little John had succeeded, through suggestion and innuendo, in planting the idea in my own mind that I could be a world record holder. He had never explicitly said it, but everyone, including me, knew that this was his plan. And so in order to make an attempt on the Channel I needed to prove myself. I needed to become more than just a student of the sport, and the baby of the gang. I needed to become a serious open water swimmer – certainly the best in the club, and one of the few people in the world who was currently capable of getting across. If I was to have any chance, Windermere must be conquered in 1987, and before my eleventh birthday, thus paving the way for a possible Channel attempt the following summer. But in truth, no one – not me, Mum, Dad or Anna, nor John himself – knew how possible this was. To our knowledge, no one had ever swum Windermere aged ten – not even Marcus.

The sun hadn't yet risen above the mountains but in the east the sky was already pale blue, its pink and red border framed by the dark ridges of the fells above us. The lake was cast in shadow along its entire length and flat calm. A mist rolled across the water's surface, thicker and fatter further offshore as the water temperature fell. From out of the mist flew a squadron of ducks. They flapped and quacked towards the shoreline breaking the silence, splashing down in loose formation and waddling ashore alongside the rowing boats, which were tied to the old jetty like wonky keys on a piano. As they landed the water lost its perfect flat gloss and a complex pattern of interlocking ripples rolled in all directions, into the mist and towards the shore. The hamlet of Lakeside on the southern tip of Windermere was being gradually woken by our presence, but it felt as if the rest of the Lake District was still fast asleep in the room next door, so we whispered.

Being greased up for the first time was an odd thing. The wax was lumpy and hard, and I felt embarrassed. John said little, but instructed me when needed. 'Tefal, you need to apply some grease to your crotch. Not my job, yours. Wear this glove, lad, take a scoop, and apply some in between your legs. Freshwater, so you don't need much.' I did as I was told, and before long the process was complete. One last ritual to observe – John used the grease to draw the number 1 on the back of my trunks – it was a visual symbol that this was my first attempt at a serious open water swim. The first of how many, I wondered.

Dennis helped load the rowing boat with the normal provisions: CB radio and car battery, a sturdy plastic box of food, hot flasks, medical supplies, a small bag for each of the crew with their waterproofs and warm layers, and my bag, with just a towel, my spare goggles and spare orange swimming hat. If things went well, I wouldn't be needing my clothes before I returned to the campsite. I was not in on the plan, though. Only John had that, somewhere in his bald and dented head.

The boat had taken on two new members. John Callaway was also a swimming coach and an old friend of John's. I knew from the brief time I had spent with him that, firstly, I liked him and, secondly, that they were very different people. 'JC' was calm and reflective while John could be volatile and irascible; JC smiled and cajoled, where John growled and instructed. I felt that JCs presence on the boat was significant – it was as if, for the first time, John had drafted in some form of help in the pursuit of his aims for the coming months. The third member of the crew was Spike, so named on account of his unusually curly hair. He was a fit and friendly teenager and a very good competitive sprint swimmer. It was not entirely clear how he had become involved here – it was often that way with people John liked – but John got on with him very well so he had become a fixture, despite a limited enthusiasm for open water swimming. He would be doing most of the rowing, I thought.

The jaw-dropping beauty of the setting made the importance of the moment more acute. The lake temperature in the middle was 57–58 degrees Fahrenheit (13–14 degrees Celsius) – another cold year following a bitter winter and a poor start to the summer. Colder than the Channel itself, and with no salt to aid buoyancy, this was a serious challenge.

John looked me in the eye. For the second time I could remember, he took both of my hands in his before he spoke, and I felt reassured. John increasingly had that effect on me. The first such occasion had occurred only recently when he took Mother Duck and me to the Netherlands for an international swimming gala, along with a coachload of swimmers from the sprint clubs in Greenwich. I had cried with homesickness, terrified at being bunked down with older kids I didn't know. As it had all come flooding out he had simply knelt down and looked me in the eye.

'Tefal. It's easy to forget sometimes that you are still a *little* Tefal. Just remember one thing. I will always, ALWAYS look after you.'

And so it had proved to be. The reassuring aspect of his personality made a timely reappearance on the shoreline that morning.

'Now, Tefal. Don't go off too quickly,' he began. 'Conditions are good, so just settle in and find your rhythm. Let's get past Storrs and up to the island first up.'

'OK, John.'

Storrs Temple lay just beyond the 4 mile point in the southern half of the lake – a Victorian folly at the end of its own causeway that jutted out from the eastern shoreline. A mile or so north was the chain ferry, then the network of islands, collectively called Belle Isle after the largest of them. If we got that far then the 4.5 miles to Ambleside was a possibility.

The duck ripples had gone so it was up to me to break the glass-like surface of the water. The mist swirled around my ankles and calves as I walked in. It was perfectly quiet as I stood in the water up to my knees. My head shook gently and involuntarily from side to side in a 'no' motion. The task in front of me was now real, and unwelcome, mostly because the water was so cold, but also because I knew that it would be horrid in the end. Horrid to push myself to the point of failure, and likely even more horrid to refuse to give in. John's voice cut the silence from the boat, which sat idle in the mist, with its two blue and white flags now hoisted but lying limp in the still air.

'Tefal, stop fannying around, will you? Let's fuckin' go, lad.' His loud voice felt like a violation of the moment and surroundings – no choice but to comply.

I swallowed my fear. If we reached Storrs in a few hours' time, the lake would have changed; there would be speedboats, sailing yachts and day-tripping steam ships plying back and forth. The wind would be up, skidding down from the fells above, teasing up the lake's surface. All stillness would be gone. But in this moment, everything was tranquil and calm, save for my heart, thudding away in my chest.

I swam off quietly, making as little splash as possible upon entry – a mark of respect to the setting. Moments later I was up with the prow of the old wooden boat, and although I could not see the effect for myself, I imagined parting the mist with my arms and bright orange rubber-lined head – a miniature icebreaker ship inching forwards on low revs.

No one on the boat was paying me any attention whatsoever, but I didn't mind. Each of them was in their own world as I studied them, busy with unspoken jobs and responsibilities. JC was on the oars. Spike was tasked to serve some tea out of one of the hot flasks. John was making notes on his clipboard as he studied the conditions around us, settling in to another long day on the lake. I felt a pang of envy; as I ventured further out into the middle and transitioned through the isotherms the lake was becoming progressively colder. The transitions between the seams of water were sudden – like flipping the temperature dial on the shower from warm to cold. I knew from my map, which

I had memorized, that in a mile or two we would enter the deepest and coldest part of the southern section. The action of the glaciers millions of years before had formed the deepest parts of the lake in the north and south sections, while the stubborn geology of the middle zone caused a network of islands to remain in situ halfway up its length.

I swam as smoothly as I could through the mist. I thought I felt the back-pressure of an eddy of water turning in the small of my back, but probably just imagined it. I concentrated on the shape of the water rolling back on itself in a circular motion as I glided gently across its surface. Underwater the scene was changing rapidly as the first of the sun's rays popped over the ridgeline. As I faced downwards and forwards, breathing out smoothly, the grease on my arms flashed bright white against the blackness of the water below. Swirling vertical blades of tiny bubbles were being formed in the wake of my forearms, and the grease was starting to form a pattern as it gradually broke down and was shaped on my skin by the repetitive angle of motion through the water. Miniature and momentary underwater shadows appeared behind my fingers and hands as they blocked the rays of sunshine, which were now being diffused into spears of light beneath the surface.

Then, almost between breaths, the mist was gone – replaced by a new texture as thousands of tiny wavelets rippled gently in the same direction. There must be the faintest of breezes. The spell had been broken and the blue and white flags began to fidget in acknowledgement.

In the above-water world there was some activity: John was bent down, rummaging below the topside of the rowing boat for something out of sight to me from the waterline. A large thermometer appeared in his hands, encased in its plastic tube. He tied it to a lanyard of bright orange string before releasing it overboard to trail a metre or two behind the boat. Was this a reaction to something I had done? I realized I was swimming faster and breathing more heavily – an automatic reflex to hitting colder water. John was paying attention.

The thermometer was retrieved after a few minutes, and a note made on the clipboard. Some ham acting began on the boat, with faces being pulled for my benefit. JC furrowed his eyebrows and made an '*Ooooooh!*' expression with his mouth, as if to convey that a moment of calamity had befallen me – the sort of wincing face you might pull when seeing someone fall off a bike. Spike did the same while wrapping his arms around himself as if to shelter from the cold. 'You're not the cold one,' I said to myself underwater. At the point John joined in the charade I gave the reaction that they always intended, and shook my head as I swam, smiling as I did so. The game was simply for them to laugh at my misfortune at being in such a cold lake in the first place, and for me to laugh back both at their teasing and at my inability to prevent it. It's quite hard to smile normally when breathing during front crawl, but the contorted change to my facial expression gave them a reaction all the same. The whole point of the exercise was to get my attention, to calm me down, and so gradually reduce my pace to be sustainable. Not a word was shared between us.

The teasing stopped, and after a few more minutes of intense swimming, I was warm again – for now at least. Slowly I let myself sink into a private world of thoughts and songs. I realized John had prepared me for this and so I welcomed the moment, in the same way I sometimes enjoyed knowingly falling asleep. I had learned that conquering the emotional isolation of long swims was the hardest part. A six hour up-and-down session on Easter Sunday in the big pool at Eltham, on my own and with no one looking on (John was in his office doing paperwork), had been particularly upsetting. In particular I remembered powerful cravings for food – an illegal Big Mac dominating the fantasy. Windermere, and the company of the boat and crew, was better by far – anything was better than six hours in the pool. It might be cold, but at least there was some company here.

A sudden roar of ear-splitting noise jolted me out of my thoughts and I swallowed water when I meant to breathe. I felt the thunder of the two fighter jets vibrate through the water as they passed overhead. Looking back, I just caught sight of them and the after-glow of their flaming engines as they zoomed southwards at a worryingly low height above the lake. I looked up at the boat for sympathy. 'Get on with it, Tefal,' was John's reply to my silent look.

. . .Then there was music to keep me company. Anna said that I was lucky to hang around with older kids, because I would know more about music, especially what was cool. By 1987 the Beastie Boys and Public Enemy had released their first albums, and acid house was creeping in at the margins of the mainstream. To have a copy on tape of any of these was to have street cred. A three-way battle between chart music, hip hop and dance was being played out daily on the minibus, but the girls, and pop, normally won. I thought this was good given that singing when swimming was more suited to melody than rap. And also because the rap stuff was hard for me to follow. The tune of the summer was already deep in my head to the point where I would sing it without even realizing: Owen Paul's 'Favourite Waste of Time'. Nothing else came close, so I sang it as I swam, and thought about Miss Piggy, because that crush was going nowhere for a while yet.

A sharp pain. Top of my right thigh but close to my hip. Like a needle being inserted. Came and went.

. . . Anna also pointed out that music and clothes were linked; hip hop fans (mostly boys) wore Adidas trainers because Run-DMC did. And thanks to Mike D, VW car badges in the car parks surrounding Windermere beauty spots were suddenly at risk of theft thanks to the enthusiasm of one of the Beastie Boys for wearing one on a chain around his neck. I often worried that

I didn't own any cool clothes but I told myself that Sergio Tacchini and Fila tracksuits were hard to get in small sizes.

The pain was back. This time it stayed. Still sharp, same place, but increasing, as if I had to do something different to release it, to make it go away. My head twisted in pain at the spasm. This must be cramp. So that's what it felt like.

'What's wrong?' said John, dropping the oars with a worried look. I had stopped swimming.

'The top of my leg hurts, John . . . quite . . . bad,' I replied with a grimace.

'Right, now listen to me,' said John calmly but firmly, the omission of my nickname making the moment more significant. 'You are doing really well . . . REALLY well,' he emphasized, 'so now I want you to kick it out for a mile. It's just a small cramp so you need to *kick it out* of your legs. It will go if you *kick it out*,' he stressed again, 'but if you don't, it will come back. Understand?'

I nodded.

'Understand?' John always demanded a reply.

'Yes.'

I wondered if the cramp was because John had altered my stroke recently. Two years ago and back in the confines of the small pool I was taught to swim with three leg kicks to every arm stroke on front crawl, but this year John had asked me to get used to kicking just one leg for every arm. He said that the power in my stroke needed to be from my arms, and that my leg kicks needed to reduce to make the stroke sustainable over long distances. Easter Sunday in the pool had been all about bedding that in, and for a long period, I found that although I needed an extra little half kick for balance as my body rotated on each arm, it suited me nicely and was indeed less tiring.

'We're at Storrs. Only a mile and a bit before Belle Isle. So let's fuckin' go, shall we?' he beamed.

With the oars still at rest and neither I nor the boat moving, my view of the surrounding lake had momentarily altered. There behind the boat, less than 100 metres away, was the angular folly of Storrs Temple, standing watchful and immovable at the end of its causeway. The little stone castle, a monument to what I had no idea, was guarding entry to all that wished to proceed north beyond it; onwards, to Belle Isle and to the middle and upper reaches of the lake. Not everyone was successful at negotiating a passage past Storrs – I thought of Bear, only last year, and, worryingly, all because of cramp.

I swam on. The Fighting Fantasy books I liked to read, in fact the only books I had the patience to read, were ones whose front cover promised 'a story where YOU become the hero'. They came with a special dice to roll at key moments, which instructed the reader which page and, ultimately after enough plays, which final outcome to turn to. It was possible to start the book many times over and read a different story every time, even if the end result was binary: live or die, victory or defeat. '*You are at the gates to Storrs Temple*,' it might have read. '*Roll the dice . . . If you roll odd, turn to section 152*' (. . .and die soon afterwards of cramp to the upper leg). '*If you roll even, turn to section 175*' (. . .and proceed past the ancient chain ferry to the mysterious Land of Belle Isle . . .). I rolled even, and followed John's additional instructions, legs re-set at 3:1, for now.

A while later the oars stopped on the boat and Spike, who faced rearwards while rowing, was looking over his shoulder. This always indicated a hazard ahead, and so I looked up and to the front on a few successive breaths to see what was going on, not breaking my stroke. The chain ferry was clanking past in front of me, and I considered the likelihood of swimming into the chain itself – a submerged tripwire. The ferry was full of cars and tourists, some of whom wore cameras around their necks, poised to capture a moment of Lakeland beauty. A young girl tugged at one of her parents and pointed at me; the adult brought up the lens and snapped me treading water as I looked back at them, waiting for the ferry to pass.

Unexpectedly the water warmed up. Long weeds reached up from the depth of the dark lake beneath and brushed my hands below the surface as I swam. The fat, slimy tentacles startled me when I first touched one. I could see a good couple of metres of their length running vertically down through the clear water, but after that they descended into blackness, to a depth I could only guess. A scene from *Star Wars* unhelpfully entered my head; the one where the heroes are enclosed in a wet tank full of space junk, while the tentacles of a submerged monster attempt to drown them by dragging them under the surface of the water. They got away with it, being Jedi, but I banished the thought all the same.

'TEEEFAL!' I heard on the next breath. I stopped swimming. 'Yes?' I replied, calling up from the water, wondering what could have caused John to interrupt the rhythm of things.

'A buoy, Tefal! . . . A buoy! Look!' he announced with glee. There, a few metres in front, was a large orange marker buoy. There were many more of them in this part of the lake but even this one would have taken some aiming at by the crew in order to have got quite so close. The buoys marked shallow water and other submerged hazards, identifying the safe channels for boats passing between the islands. This one, like most, was covered in white and black bird shit. The white stuff was the fresh shit. The black stuff was the ever-accumulating undercoat. What followed had become a drill – but not one I liked. I said nothing and simply swam forwards to the large orange ball. I butted it gently with my forehead, hoping this would look like the act of humiliation it was supposed to be from behind. 'NO, TEFAL!' shouted John. 'You need to actually KISS the buoy . . . You *know* the rules.' Unable and unwilling to protest, I kissed the thing. It was slimy and firm. I looked back, to check I had passed the test. The crew were rolling with laughter. John waved me away with some urgency as Spike picked up the oars, so I resumed, shoulders aching.

There was no one there at Belle Isle. I sat in the water up to my chest alongside the rowing boat. John handed me a jam sandwich, Roberts's strawberry on thick white bread. I ate it quickly. There was a plastic thermos-lid cup of milky sweet tea. As I sipped it the warmth of the liquid felt as if a hot water pipe running through my body had been turned on. It was the most intense feeling of relief I had ever experienced. The chocolate digestives came next, then a refill of the tea.

'How are you feeling?' asked John.

'OK,' I said evenly. Each syllable of the word came out of my mouth slower than I had expected. They sounded sluggish. Perhaps I was colder than I had thought in my core, but I was not *really* cold. I didn't want to say much else anyway. Because I was upset.

'Are you cold?' asked John after a pause.

'Erm . . . No. Not really,' I said honestly, again sounding a little simple as my lips struggled to wrap themselves around the words. '. . . Not cold.' I left something hanging.

'What is it then, Tefal? Why are you *sulking*?' asked John, a note of provocation in his tone.

I chewed on the remnants of the second digestive, impervious to the insult.

'Where is everybody?' I said, as fast as my lips allowed, which was slowly.

'They're not here. You won't see them until we reach the end.'

I chewed some more.

'Why not?' Some biscuit crumbs spilled from my numb lips into the water.

John held the rail of the boat and leaned in to me, locked his eyes on mine. 'Because we are an hour early, Tefal, that's why,' he said quietly, and smiled.

'Tefal, stay with the FUCKIN' boat, will you? For fuck's sake!' Some time, probably an hour or more, had passed, but my condition had deteriorated quickly. I was well past my cold and distance threshold and experiencing the darkest side of long distance swimming for the first time. I didn't reply because I couldn't speak. The boat had veered back towards me to re-establish the appropriate distance between us, and so taken itself from the line of shortest distance to the end point. I had to follow the boat, not the other way round, otherwise we would certainly fail. We resumed.

Clunk.

'Shit,' I mumbled underwater, opening my eyes once more, this time in sudden pain. I had swum underneath the oar and taken a knock to the head. It hurt. Spike should have held the stroke out of the water but probably took his eye off me for a moment. We had been out there for hours now so I couldn't blame him. Things were unravelling. I was very cold. I looked up to see if we had passed the White Hotel in what felt like the last hour. There it sat on the eastern shore, unmoved, staring back at me obstinately. In that moment the tears came. This was the moment then. To give up.

John intervened, hoping to regain some control.

'Tefal. Listen to me, lad. You are a mile and a half from Ambleside.' I shook my head in reply as I bobbed alongside the boat. John could see I was crying, rather than making any attempt to speak.

'Look up,' he commanded instead, and pointed northwards. I could see the masts and rooftops of Ambleside again, just like last year. A chocolate digestive was retrieved from the plastic box and tossed into the lake for me to eat. Like a desperate duck in the park I grabbed for it before it sank, and ate it down.

A mile and a half then. I decided I was going in. It would be horrible but, stroke by stroke, I was going in.

That night I sat in the deckchair reserved for the swimmer for just the second time as we all gathered in the food tent for dinner, still tinned mince, fresh mash and tinned marrowfat peas, with creamed rice for pudding too. Only now was I returning to a reasonably alert state of mind. It was taking a long time for the effects of the swim to leave me, even though I had been out of the water for six hours. Not so much the cold, because I was warm now, but more the effect on my brain, only just resuming normal operating speed after what I now knew to be six hours and five minutes of solitude and cold immersion.

From the atmosphere in the tent I knew the swim had created a moment. It was as if no one knew quite what to say. John was quiet and stern faced, and we mostly ate in silence. Anna was being gently teased for having cried with happiness as I landed.

John sent everyone to bed as dusk crept across the evening summer sky. He held me back in the tent, so it was just the two of us. We walked up to the wash block together. Despite the day's events the natural routine of the campsite would continue. Very soon all would be silent, apart from the occasional bleat of a sheep, or the sound of any rain or wind that decided to visit. It looked like a quiet clear night, so the stars would be bright.

'I need to keep you up a little longer, Tefal. Sorry, lad. I know you're tired.' The walk to the wash block was proving a challenge. I felt John's arm around my shoulder, steadying me as I laboured up the path. I realized we had *both* achieved something today.

'Don't worry, John,' I said, enjoying the moment of his company, and of feeling special.

'It's a safety precaution. I won't let you sleep for some hours after a very long swim, just so as you are certain to wake up, you see,' he said in a matter of fact way.

'I know,' I said, despite not knowing the medical reason for this. It was an accepted 'club fact' that you mustn't let a swimmer sleep after a long cold swim – just in case something caused them not to wake up at all. Besides, I was enjoying the time with him, even though he still seemed a little solemn. I wanted John to be happy, and when I did something to please him, I found it made me happy too.

'Tefal, well done today,' he said as we strolled slowly up the path. I nodded, not quite knowing how to reply. 'Thanks' sounded a bit cocky, so I said nothing.

'You know this is quite a big deal, right?' he enquired gently.

'Yes, I think so,' I replied this time. 'Does it mean that I might swim the Channel, John?'

He paused. 'Yes. Yes, it does,' he said, looking down at the gravel track as we walked slowly side by side. 'Maybe, and it's just a maybe, as soon as next year.'

I knew exactly what that meant, and I knew John knew that I knew. An excited grin crept across my face that I could neither conceal nor hold in. In that moment John told me, for the first time explicitly, that I might have the chance to break the world record for the youngest conqueror – to break Marcus's record. Until this point everything had been oblique; speculation by others, the subtle placement of the idea by John – a kind of psychological seeding process that left me initially curious, then flattered, and finally ambitious. He caught my expression as he looked sideways at me and his tone instantly hardened.

'But you are NOT to get big-'eaded about it, Tefal, do you hear me?' he blurted out as if releasing pent-up anger. 'I won't have you swaggering around, thinking you own the place, and making a tit of yourself.' 'Do you hear? It's not gonna happen, so you better watch yerself.'

'OK, John,' I said, stone-faced and serious. But inside I was skipping.

*

I wore my new sunglasses, the ones I had bought from Dickinson's Chemist with my pocket money. They were Tom Cruise-style *Top Gun* glasses. The lenses were a bit big for my face, but I thought my head would probably grow into them soon enough. I added a sweat band around my brow to copy Pat Cash, who had recently beaten Ivan Lendl in the Wimbledon final. I wore my new white Fred Perry polo shirt – real logo, not fake – and, above all, my new prized Adidas trainers. They were the basic and cheapest ones, but the fact that Mum had bought them at all, not to mention the Fred Perry, was a result. Three stripes and tennis logos counted. I looked in the mirror, smiled, and walked off to the pools. It was Wednesday night – club night.

The Windermere swimmers and this year's two relay teams, both of which once again included Anna, were in cold water still, so there was no swimming to be done indoors, but hopefully a bit of coaching for a younger group from the poolside. What I really wanted was to see my swimming friends, and for other people to ask me about my Windermere success. I would thank them politely, I thought; tell them that it was very hard but that I just had to hang in there until the end. If they asked about my great outfit, well, that was no big deal.

There was a copy of the newspaper lying on the table where the swimmers signed in. It had been left open on the right page, with my photo (an embarrassing one that had been taken recently by the *Eltham Times*) staring back at me. There was a short article that relayed the fact that a ten-year-old London boy had swum Lake Windermere, in what was thought to be a record for age, and that he had plans to swim the Channel and so mount a world record attempt the following year. None of this was news to me, so I didn't really react when I read it for the first time with others looking on. I was shocked to see it was the *London Evening Standard*, though. That was a pretty big paper.

'I'm famous!' I said as I looked up smiling to the surrounding cabal of parents and swimmers. There was no reply as such, perhaps a few nods of the head as they passed on through. People wandered off to get changed, or to watch their kids swim from the side. I coached some six to eight year olds for an hour on widths. One of them was really good.

'Tefal,' began John curtly from his office chair a couple of hours later. He sat behind his large desk, looking a little angry, which was not unusual towards the end of a Wednesday night. It was late and I had bounded into the office, excited at all that had happened, but also excited to see him . . . to see John.

'Hi, John!' I replied chirpily.

'Tefal,' he repeated. He paused momentarily when he saw my outfit (sunglasses now resting on my head) and gave a confused and disapproving look, before resuming. 'I am sending you to Coventry,' he said, before looking back down at his papers.

'Oh right. Why Coventry?' I asked happily in return, willing to comply but a little confused. My mind raced over the possibilities. I knew roughly where it was – further north, but not so far as the Lakes. We had only last Easter spent a day and night in Coventry on a family canal boat holiday. Still I was clueless, but John didn't answer.

'How come Coventry, John?' I repeated, eager to understand the plan. 'Is there a special pool there? Or a lake?'

Still no answer. In fact, he didn't even look up, which was strange. Something was wrong. I stood there awkwardly. No explanation was forthcoming.

'John?' I waited.

I knew he could hear me.

'John!' I demanded. Still he didn't reply.

None of this made sense. I felt a wave of emotion bubble up inside, and my face reddened. I could feel myself about to cry.

'John?' I asked gently, quietly, *pleadingly* for a final time as the tears came to the surface. Nothing.

I ran out of the office and looked for the nearest escape route. The stairs down to the underground men's changing area for the big pool were close by and the big pool was now closed for the evening. I hurried down into the cave, found an empty unlit cubicle and sobbed.

It was a few minutes before I was ready to come out. I had done something terrible and I didn't know what it was. I had angered John, the person I most wanted to please, and to the point where he had shut me off entirely and wanted to send me away to another city. I looked in the mirror. My eyes were puffy and red. People would know that I had been crying, the worst thing. But I had to get up top and find Dad so we could go home. I resolved to hold it all in, and act my way out of the situation. No more crying.

I saw Dad and promptly burst into tears again. He bent down and gave me the cuddle of a confused and concerned parent. I felt like a little child, not a ten-year-old lake-conqueror. 'What is it, son? What's happened?'

'John says he's sending me to Coventry, and I don't know why, because he won't tell me . . .' I sobbed. 'He is refusing to say anything at all!' I spluttered.

'All right, all right,' Dad soothed and cuddled, 'don't worry, Tom. You're not going to Coventry . . . It's OK.'

'But why Coventry, Dad? I don't understand.'

'It's an expression. It means he isn't talking to you. Have you done something to upset him?'

'No. Don't think so.'

Anna appeared, looking worried. 'Where have you been?' she chipped in. 'I've been looking for you everywhere.'

'Not saying,' I sobbed, deciding to conceal all unnecessary information in self-defence, even against my sister.

'What's going on here?' Dad asked Anna, clearly detecting she held some additional information.

Anna handed him what was now a roughly torn cutting (by

her own hand) from the *Evening Standard*. Dad looked at it quizzically. 'Not sure I understand. So what?' he challenged.

'John's not happy about it,' Anna replied neutrally. There was clearly another circle of information to which Anna had access but I did not.

'Is that right?' said Dad, in a way that suggested he was trying to control his voice. 'Wait here, you two,' he said firmly. Anna looked at me with a face full of worry. This was not good. We followed as close behind as we dared as Dad approached John's open door and presented himself. From a safe distance I could see that strong words were being exchanged, then the door closed, and Dad went inside the office.

A couple of minutes later he emerged. Stern-faced and resolute. 'Let's go.' Dad was rarely very strict about anything. We left in silence.

Dad came up to see me in bed that night and tuck me in; a rarity these days. He sat on my bed and patiently outlined what he thought had happened. He explained John's concerns, which must have been shared earlier behind the closed office door; that he was worried I was becoming too cocky – becoming a big-head. He explained that John had not agreed to the *Evening Standard* article being printed, and had thought Dad had sent the material, which both of us knew not to be true, in fact absurd – a point Dad had made to John. That mystery would remain unsolved, but the wider problem, of my recent attitude, was still in question.

'What shall I do?' I asked.

'Well, I have arranged with John that you both need to cool off for a bit – let things calm down. And then to speak to one another about it, sensibly, next time you go to training. So that is an option open to you if you choose.' Typically Dad had found a way out for both sides – no wonder he was a solicitor. 'But I do need to ask you something myself, Tom,' he said, looking slightly uneasy. I looked back at him, expectantly.

'Is this what you want to do? To swim, with John as your coach?' Dad looked at me as I pondered the question. I had never really thought about it. I was used to doing everything John asked of me, and willingly, no matter what it was or how hard. I always wanted to please him, to earn his respect. It hadn't really occurred to me that there was actually a choice.

He continued, 'You see, I don't know anything about swimming, but I can see that John Bullet is a brilliant coach, and a very talented man. He is also sometimes . . . a difficult man. I learned that for myself tonight.' This was a serious intervention. He went on . . .

'I do think he wants the very best for you, so on that basis *we* are willing for this to carry on.' He emphasized 'we' to underline his own control of the matter. 'But on the strict proviso that *you* actually want to do this. If you do, we will support you. But you will need to understand all that comes with it. And that includes John, his methods, and I suspect a few more tears on the way. And if you don't want to do it, well, that's fine, and fine by your mum too.' I knew the last part alluded to the fact that Mum, once the driving force of the swimming idea, had become more uncomfortable with the plans that were now unfolding.

I lay in silence and processed the advice, even though the answer was already glaringly obvious. After a pause I replied.

'Of course I want to do it, Dad. I want to break the record. I want to be the youngest person to swim the English Channel.'

'I thought you might say that,' he chuckled. 'Now get some sleep.'

Feeling better, I did as I was told. But not before drawing back the curtains and pulling the sash window next to my bed wide open – to let in the cool night air.

JC appeared back on the rail. Things had been going well, for a while. He unwrapped another Chupa Chups lollipop and began teasing me once more. But I didn't really feel like reacting this time. The last hour, maybe even two by now, had passed slowly even though I had swum hard. Buoyed by the prospect of success, and with some soup to burn inside, I had made a renewed effort. This was the part of the swim where I would break my own time and distance record and so the deductions ran over and over in my head. The minimum known distance for a swim crossing of the Channel was thought to be about 28 miles, on account of the tides. If I was now over halfway, and six or seven hours in, then I must have swum at least 14 miles of the minimum 28. But how much more, hour by hour, was what mattered now. I somehow needed to find at least another 14 miles from my body; another length and a half of Windermere.

The constant reworking of the calculations in my head triggered something else; I kept looking up to see the coast, and to see if it looked any closer since the last time I looked up. But it never looked closer, and so I started to look more and more in growing desperation. The physical act was becoming almost involuntary, like a yawn or a sneeze, and was disrupting my stroke, preventing me from making the progress that would bring the cliffs any closer. I began to feel a desperate anger at my situation and the resulting conversation I had with myself became an outlet. This was fucking impossible.

JC sucked his lollipop and pulled a face. 'Fucker. He knows that will piss me off. JC is a fucker.' He didn't let the lollipop tease go for ages. Then a smug wave. A comedic grin. Each act dragged out over a minute or two, making me angrier. At one point he hid, only to reappear a stroke or two later. The behaviour was strange even for him, so I kept watching for the next instalment. Eventually, somehow, he made me laugh. He saw the contorted smile on my face as I took a breath and folded his arms in triumph. I had not looked up to see England for at least twenty minutes.

Things continued like that for a while. Meanwhile, the pain

was accumulating all the time. My body was in new territory. The soreness was acute; the feeling of the shoulder blades rubbing together abrasively on every stroke was building, beyond what I had experienced before. The burning discomfort in my thighs and hips was increasing too. If I managed to block out the sensation of one, the other took over. Pain cues more anger. Where the fuck were we anyway? I had been focused on managing the pain for some time, so maybe we were closer.

At last, John held up the bottle. It wasn't red. Must be chicken soup. I swam over and repeated the drill. But I knew this was going to be a different conversation. Because I wanted to give up.

'How are you?'

'Tired. My legs reel hurt. I . . . I have a problem . . . with my shoulds . . .' The words were not coming out right, but at least I could tell.

'Tefal, listen to me.'

'Why?' I replied out loud. I was preparing my brain to stop swimming and to give up.

'*Listen* to me, Tefal. Because you have ten miles to go. Ten miles.'

This time I did want to cry. Things felt desperate *now*, yet there was still so much to do. Ten fucking miles. John was being straight with me, because he expected me to be able to deal with it, and probably because he felt there was no alternative. I searched. There was silence between us for a while as I bobbed up and down. Another way of looking at it, was that I was probably two-thirds of the way there, give or take the odd mile. I swigged the chicken soup and considered the options. Inside I knew the truth, which was that I *could* carry on swimming. I just didn't want to because I was exhausted and because it was painful. But if I was two-thirds of the way there, then perhaps I had to keep trying. The thought of climbing onto the boat and facing John and the crew having given up was equally unhappy. For now there was no option. In fact, I realized that even entertaining the idea there was an option at all was dangerous. It was a battle I would eventually lose by giving in, only then to regret it immediately afterwards.

I finished the soup and threw the bottle into the sea. I thought about it sinking all the way down to the bottom of the English Channel and wondered how long it would take to reach the seabed. I had no idea how deep the water was. What was the seabed like anyway? Some fish, lots of sand and no light probably. My brain was wandering off, even when I was treading water and supposed to be speaking to John.

'Can I have a biscuit?' I snapped out of the trance.

'Yes, Tefal.' John lobbed another chocolate digestive overboard and I grabbed it from the surface before it sank.

'How far to go?' I asked, even though he had only just told me. I had to hear him say it again, and I wanted just a few more seconds of rest before resuming. Then I noticed the doctor on the rail for the first time, looking at me carefully. What the fuck did that ginger-bearded twat want? This had nothing to do with him.

'About ten miles,' repeated John, and sensing something else, this time he carried on. 'We are still on for a really good time. You've just got to stick at it. Listen to me now. The next couple of hours are going to be the hardest. You will be going through a barrier, but you are just going to have to get through it.' He spoke slowly and clearly. The chopping hand was there, but I had to really concentrate to process the information. A 'barrier'. We had discussed this at various points in the past year or two. John had talked about any swimmer reaching a low point in a solo attempt of the Channel. It could be overcome, but the overwhelming majority failed to do so. Something about the way he described it sounded mystical, as if no one really knew why it happened or how to prevail, but it was inevitable no matter who was involved or the preparations they had endured.

'Do you want another biscuit?' asked John after a pause.

'No. Fine thanks.' I swam on.

5. *The Early Starter*

2.15 p.m., 6 September 1988 – 9 hours, 7 miles off the English coast, English Channel

I lurched out of my trance and rolled onto my back. Something was trying to attack me. It had gone for my legs and so I kicked it away. As I rolled over the noise it made was terrifying. A drone-like siren of . . .

Then there was nothing there. Breathless in the water, I tried to process the information. I looked up at the boat, only half comprehending the scene or the people on board.

'Calm down. Calm down! It's OK, Tefal.' Mother Duck was on the rail watching over me, on duty. 'You just hit a big patch of seaweed, that's all,' she called out. The taste in my mouth was more foul than saline. Like petrol. The seaweed must have trapped fuel spill from a ship.

'What's that noise?' I said drunkenly.

'It's nothing to worry about – just the Goodwin lightship. We're close by.'

Treading water for a moment, I realized the sound was loud but occasional – like an industrial fog horn, despite there being no fog. I had heard of Goodwin Sands. It was mentioned in the same conversations as a place called Sandettie. Both were shallow points in the sea, and to be avoided. Swimmers needed to time their tides and routes in order to do so, or else their support ships would run aground. This was one of the reasons why a proper pilot was required. According to John, you needed special knowledge and years of experience to successfully escort a

Channel swimmer. It was not the first loud noise to have shaken me on the crossing. Some hours earlier a hovercraft had buzzed past on its way from Ramsgate or Dover. I had never seen one up close on the move. It was loud and fast – an awesome sight from the water. Coming back into full consciousness caused another rush of pain. I needed to find a deeper state.

Five months before then I had woken cold. The window in my bedroom was wide open, and the single bedsheet I was allowed for warmth wasn't having the required effect. My room was small, my bed taking up half the floor space. It was a clear night in April. I drew the bedsheet over my head, pulled it tight and began to breathe heavily into what became a makeshift tent. If I made an 'ooohhh' shape with my mouth and focused on the 'h' of 'ooohhh', the breath seemed to be warmer, and if I did that enough – a few minutes or more – the temperature inside the bedsheet tent would warm a fraction, allowing me to go back to sleep. It never occurred to me to close the window – that would be to disobey the new instructions.

It was now 1988, and I was officially in training to break the world record, and these were the new rules. No duvets, just a sheet – windows always open. No hot showers, nor baths; t-shirts allowed, of course, but no jumpers. Not even if it snowed. Certainly no coats. Then there was a new diet, designed to make me fat – my body was another weapon to counter the conditions. For endurance, there was a childhood's worth of swimming to be done, in just a few months. And finally, there was *me*: how I thought and responded to things, and so a lot of talking, with John, to be done in the margins.

1988 was a big year for Eltham Training and Swimming Club. It was the twenty-first anniversary year of the club's formation, and John Bullet had big plans. John always had big plans, but these were bigger than normal. Anna and cousin Vicky were selected to be part of the team for the club's first ever two-way Channel relay attempt; same rules – a team of six on hour-long stints – just double the challenge and then some. There was now talk of a Junior Relay, for a team all under the age of fourteen, but at this stage the membership of that squad was far from clear. It was also now obvious that Mother Duck, after years of self-preparation on the one hand, and the nurturing of the rest of us on the other, would attempt a solo crossing herself for the first time. Then there was me. This was less talked about – in front of me at least – but everyone knew it was happening. There was a world record for the taking and John had set his sights on it. As had I.

The swimming club itself had been John's own creation, according to Anna. It was unclear when he had decided to focus on Channel Swimming, but the albums and notice boards hinted at a journey of discovery through the 1970s and early 1980s, with black and white press cuttings of groups of teenagers in flares tallying up ever more relay swims. The first successful relay swim was in 1972. The successful soloists and Marcus's world record of nine years ago were still the crowning achievements, but the club had grown steadily under John's stewardship, and so had its collective ambitions. It had become a community, and for its members more of a movement than a club. In the world of elite swimming, though, and despite our own confidence in ourselves, we were seen as outsiders – a motley crew of cocky South-East London kids, led by an eccentric and irascible talisman in John. I didn't care about that. I just wanted to swim. And to spend more time with John. As 1988 unfolded, we spent more time together than ever, and I was happy.

I watched out of the window for the dark blue Vauxhall Cavalier. It was the newer model of the exact same car John had before. In fact, this was his third dark blue Vauxhall Cavalier in a row. As he arrived I grabbed my swimming bag from the hallway and called out to Mum as I left. I threw my kit onto the back seat, jumped in the front, and put my seatbelt on. It was early, 8 o'clock, on a bright Sunday morning.

'Where are we going, then?' I asked.

'For a drive. I thought we might get some breakfast. Good idea, Young Tefal?'

'Suits me,' I replied, wondering, perhaps hoping since it was Sunday, if the swimming bag on the back seat would even be needed. Barely anything was said for the next thirty minutes. I went to turn up a song I recognized on the radio and John told me not to touch the dials. John listened to Radio 2, but I was not a fan – too much weird music, sometimes even country music, which according to Anna was just plain wrong. We drove down the M2 until we reached a turnoff nearer to Dover than London. This Little Chef was John's favourite. He only ever ate in Little Chefs when on the road. In the last year we had stopped off, once or twice, just the two of us, for a bite to eat. John always paid, because I had no money. I always thanked him, to be polite, realizing that he often treated me to things that he ought not to have paid for.

'Morning, Mave!' he called out to a buxom lady in her Little Chef pinafore. 'Hello, John,' she replied tunefully as she bustled busily towards us, bumping into the identical bench tables as she went. She wore a Little Chef name badge bearing her actual name – Mavis.

We took our seats next to the window and watched the cars and lorries whizzing down the motorway. Sitting opposite one another in silence, we studied the traffic.

'Who's this young man then?' asked Mavis as she flipped open her order pad and clicked the top of the biro into action.

'This is Tefal,' replied John.

'Tefal, eh? Why Tefal?' she asked with an inquisitive smile in my direction.

'I've got a big spam,' I said matter-of-factly, pointing slightly to my forehead as I said it.

'I see,' she said, wearing an expression that suggested the opposite.

'Two Early Starters, please, Mave. With tea, and white toast,' directed John. I nodded my agreement at Mave, smiling smugly to prove that John and I were of the same mind on absolutely everything. She scribbled on the pad, and left us alone. Early Starter . . . I liked the name of this signature Little Chef dish. It was reserved for people like me. Well, John and me at any rate. It was now May and during the preceding winter I had been swimming before school most mornings and so now considered myself an early starter. Dad would drive me to the pool in the dark and cold, normally in his pyjamas, before returning to pick me up on his way to work. A 6.30 dropoff meant I could do at least an hour's up and down while John did paperwork in the office. The lifeguards wouldn't arrive until I had left for school, so I had the big pool all to myself.

The next conversation over our breakfast would be about tea, since John could drink tea at a remarkably hot temperature. I could not because I was eleven, John would say. 'When you're older it's easier to drink hot tea.' Comforting to know. It was nearly always a point of discussion, another part of our new routine. Other frequent conversations covered the merits of Vauxhall cars, the reasons why everyone should be made to take life-saving classes, and, more often these days, the complexities of long distance swimming – tides, pilotage and endurance.

The Little Chef-branded plates arrived, identically loaded with a full English, just as the photo on the menu had promised. Mavis brought the toast, pre-buttered, and finally the tea, in two stubby silver teapots that dribbled when tipped over the white cup and saucer. The cups boasted the familiar logo – the chubby cartoon chef with his hat on. So did the paper napkins, carpets and the sugar sachets. I only took sugar in tea during a long cold swim, like John. This was the Little Chef routine: logo propaganda and cloned conformity on a plate. It was a drill of repetition and regularity, designed to generate trust, to keep the customer coming back. It resembled the relationship that had emerged between John and me.

In the space of less than four years the swimming club had taken over nearly every aspect of our lives, but there were no objections from Anna and me. To pay for a new bus John needed to raise money, so evenings after school were spent collecting old newspapers house-to-house in Eltham to sell for recycling. Spare Sundays in the winter had been given over to life-saving classes, open to the general public and run by John for a fee. Boot sales, sponsored walks to Dover, club discos and 'horse race nights' completed the endless carousel. Anna said it wasn't just about the bus; Channel swims cost money, as did the camps. The club was about participation as much as ability, and the fundraising meant everyone could join in.

Weekend Dover training camps were becoming more frequent and more intense and the spirit of the group was rising. A new cohort of younger swimmers was coming through as part of the Junior Relay idea. It included Rabbit (buck teeth), Pauline (a boy named Paul), Tubbs (well fed), Bushy (eyebrows) and 'MDJ' – Mother Duck Junior (Kirstin, but clearly someone marked out as a future leader). Rabbit, whose real name was Andrew, had become my best friend in the club; we were the same age, lived close by in Eltham and he could make anyone laugh on demand. He was also very kind. With its new members the squad was a mixture of seasoned veterans and novice would-be Channel aspirants. After three years I no longer felt like the baby of the gang. I had outgrown that role in swimming terms, and so had a new role to play encouraging others.

Dad's prediction from two years prior had come to pass and our cherished lido had closed down over the winter, so John also had to find a solution to our training needs. The South-East London Aquatic Centre in Woolwich became known to us by its acronym – SELAC. Aquatic Centre was a mild overstatement of its current re-purposing but an understatement of its past use. The pair of old dry docks, known to the locals as Henry's docks, were built for ship construction on the banks of the Thames by Henry VIII. But they no longer matched their surroundings, dwarfed by high rise council flats on three sides. A weed-strewn concrete surface divided them. The building that lay in between, already derelict, was quite new – early 1980s, I thought – its intended purpose not entirely clear. We decided it was for the sub-aqua divers who came to explore the depths, though not many of them came. Around the perimeter a high security fence kept people away, but the residents of the surrounding flats could look down on us all the while.

The smaller of the two docks was given over to coarse fishing and allowed to become overgrown with weeds. Dicky and Giant joked that the weed the fishermen were enjoying smelt quite good. The larger dock was full of cold, clean freshwater and, importantly, was about 100 metres long. When we first arrived John posted sentries around the place, having arranged for an extra watch of older Seniors and parents to help manage any interference from troublemakers who might throw stones, or worse. I got the sense that we ought not to have been there at all. I wondered if John was taking a calculated and necessary risk, because there was no choice – not this year.

The enormous steps that cascaded from each side to form the 'V' were 'listed' for historical reasons, according to Dad. I tried to imagine the dock when empty, with the hulk of a great wooden ship filling the void as tiered armies of men stood on levels either side working on the hull. Perhaps that's why the divers came – to look for historical artefacts, gold coins and skeletons.

Some nights, on a high tide, the Woolwich ferry would moor

itself just on the other side of the dock wall. When the light across the Thames was just right the view was stunning; over on the Isle of Dogs some huge buildings were rising from the ground and starting to dominate the skyline. Canary Wharf was to be a major development, the biggest of the office blocks being billed as the highest in Europe, Dad said. SELAC had become our new midweek cold-water home, and even though Anna and I still mourned the loss of our treasured lido in Eltham Park, I was growing to like it. It was a bigger pool, and a new routine for a bigger year. But it was no Windermere.

After a swim of around seven and a quarter hours and 15.5 miles on the lake that summer, I strode out of the water at Belle Isle in reasonable nick. That single moment of success finally confirmed the plan: I would make an attempt on the Channel no later than 9 October, in a bid for the world record. I knew from talking with John that the window for the season was driven largely by temperature; the Channel takes a long time to warm up over summer, but holds warmer water until quite late on, before a dramatic autumnal correction. Save for any deliberations by the Channel Swimming Association, which still had to authorize my attempt, this was now all too real. But the summer holiday that bridged the gap between Windermere and the day of reckoning was a hinterland, and some even more peculiar routines became normal.

'You're not to go out, Tefal. Not during the day, not without my permission. Understand, lad? Unless you are training with me, it ain't happening,' John had instructed.

'But what will I do all day?' I remonstrated.

'Eat, preferably. And watch telly, lots and lots of telly,' came the reply, accompanied by a toothy grin.

I followed it to the letter. Breakfast was a self-catered affair. A whole tin of Heinz beans, three scrambled eggs and two thick slices of buttered bread. Just like swimming camp, but cooked by my own hand rather than Mother Duck's. More complex was the porridge starter. It had to have a full dessertspoon of soya flour added, why I never found out. Lunch was normally more creative. I had full access to the kitchen and any provisions Mum chose to supply me with. Homemade bread, pizzas, pies and even the odd cake were all suddenly within my repertoire, largely thanks to a lady called Delia Smith who appeared on the front of a large black cookbook in the kitchen, holding an egg. Mum groaned at the mess, but presumably this was better than having to churn out such nutritional excellence herself. Dinner was her domain anyway. John had insisted on liver once a week, shepherd's pie twice a week, and steak just the once. The rising food bill was a cause of marital discussion. Dad was allowed to keep his 'fish and chip Friday' routine with Nick the Greek, much to everyone's relief.

Week by week it was working – I was getting fatter. Fit but fat, and, more importantly, buoyant. Having gained a stone or more in weight over the summer (I was nearly as heavy in stone as my age in years), and having not been near hot water in six months, I had an outside chance of staying warm.

Eat, swim, eat, swim, eat. Repeat. Richie Benaud kept me company for large swathes of the day, as the BBC brought the full depressing picture of a day's play against the West Indies into the sitting room. I sat and watched on my own, hoping Anna might return from her daily boy-chase to liven things up. She rarely did.

Summer nights training with the Channel squad were a high point, partly because I craved the company of my swimming friends, and John. The drive from Eltham Baths to Woolwich took me past Shooters Hill and our old house, the common, my old nursery school and the magnificent barracks. I looked out for soldiers, and guns, and always felt a twinge of excitement as we drove past.

The musical diet that summer was happily more varied. The

charts were under an unwelcome assault from Stock, Aitken and Waterman's 'Hit Factory', and a series of novelty records designed to annoy rather than satisfy, and so albums were getting a look in on the minibus stereo. Run-DMC had released *Tougher Than Leather*, and the opening track, 'Run's House', was played loudly as we exited Eltham for the banks of the Thames. Anna kept a copy of the *Dirty Dancing* soundtrack close to hand – there were classic soul tracks mixed in with some decent US pop; nothing to upset anyone. The mix tape left over from Windermere had some highlights among the crap, but the song that made everyone look out the window and reflect was by Michael Jackson. 'Man in the Mirror' made us stop and think.

Most of us saw that 1988 was already special no matter what came next, and that together we were sharing a time that would define us. We knew we were in a generation of swimmers that could write the next chapter of club history, and that song seemed to catch our shared mood, and fondness for one another.

It was a good night for swimming by the Thames. Clear summer skies and late evening light made our dock and the surrounding city a thing of beauty. The sunset was reflecting off the newly installed glass of the Canary Wharf tower, the ambient light causing our surroundings to remind me of a well-baked golden cake. I swam hard. The tunes playing in my head were uplifting: 'Rush Hour' by Jane Wiedlin, 'Crash' by the Primitives and 'A Little Respect' by Erasure. Plumes of bubbles rose from the deep divers below, adding to the drama. My energy levels rose to keep pace with the music playing in my head. Turning against the dock wall I picked out a swimmer in front, the further away the better, and made a plan to chase them down. I had begun to do this a couple of years before in the big pool on Wednesday nights, and I was happiest when the plan resulted in the narrowest of victories as the target swimmer (who was unaware and so never to be upset) and I touched the far end within a second or less of each other. It rarely worked when I tried it on Anna. She was too quick.

Midway through a pursuit I caught sight of Rabbit, on the edge of the dock, and in trouble. He was cold, which was not unusual, but had also developed a severe leg cramp and so was trying to get out, labouring awkwardly up the giant steps as he did so. His right leg was locked out, as if in a brace. Once he reached the terrace he hobbled, shaking violently from the cold, towards the stash of kit bags. John, unusually quiet that night, caught sight of him and walked over briskly. His face was all rage. He pushed Rabbit back into the water. There was some shouting. I stopped swimming instantly and looked on, treading water from the middle. In four years I had never seen John lose his cool. In fact, apart from the odd pool-based mass-wrestle during free time, I had never seen him lay a hand on anyone, let alone push someone into the water. A commotion unfolded between them as Rabbit tried to explain, this time from the water, that he couldn't go on. John swore and shouted, waved his arms around in anger, and then stormed off. Mother Duck swam over, helped Rabbit from the dock and calmed things down. John disappeared.

The strain of the summer of 1988 had reached fever pitch. John was under enormous pressure, albeit largely self-induced. I knew from Windermere that he had an extraordinary ability to function without much sleep, even though he insisted others must not. But he was effectively working seven days a week: opening the pool at 6 a.m., running the large public baths all day long, and training us in the evenings. On his days off, he was with me, Mother Duck or both, doing yet more training. He was masterminding a golden year: two solo swims including a world record attempt, and two relays – one of them the renowned two-way. The burden was starting to show.

'All right, Rabs?' I said, dripping over my kit bag thirty minutes later, eager to find my towel. He sat against the wall. The colour had returned to his face but his lips remained blue and he was still shaking a little. He was wrapped in even more clothing than usual.

'OK, Teefs?' He looked up smiling. 'All good here, mate,' he added unconvincingly. 'What about old JB busting me back in then, eh?' he said, his jokey demeanour masking a deeper wound.

'Yeah, mate. I saw it. You did your best. That's all.'

'I just get so f-fucking *cold*, mate, n-no matter how . . . f-fast I go,' he said, a hint of panic entering his voice, replacing its normal comedic timbre. Rabbit of all people didn't want to let anyone down. Relay squads relied on pace to beat the tide, which he had – but the cold was another thing entirely. It was a problem with no obvious solution. I was angry with John – he had upset my friend, who was doing his best. It was John who had put him in this position in the first place, I thought. The pressure was starting to show, the cracks in people's resilience appearing, John included.

'Well, look on the bright side, mate. At least you're not a big fat "Mr Lard Body", eh?' I said, grabbing a handful of my copious belly blubber and wobbling it in his face, hoping somehow to cheer him up. He laughed his usual laugh and things resumed as normal.

Two weeks before the return to school I was back at the Little Chef to see Mave, en route to Dover with John, but also with Mother Duck. The call had come the night before to be ready in the morning with my swimming kit, and my passport. Initially I panicked, but John explained on the phone that this was not the day of the swim. It was a special trip, for just the three of us, to take a look at the French coast and enjoy a day out together. From the rail of the ferry's top deck Clair, now twenty-two, and I looked back to England, and forwards to France – both of which could be seen from the middle – and considered the massive undertaking that we were trying to attempt. The great expanse of the Dover Strait stretched out in all directions. Sensing my apprehension, John was playful and made jokes all day at the expense of us both.

We drove to Wissant Bay in the August sunshine. Mother Duck and I put our arms around each other on the cliff top as John took a photo on her camera for her album. 'My God, you two are ugly,' he said, releasing the shutter. We rolled our eyes and laughed. Behind us was the English Channel, which we both hoped to conquer. In front of us, holding the camera, stood the man who, remarkably and in just three years in my case, had planted the seed of an idea, nurtured it into reality and then made it possible. The beach below was windy and with some surf to play in, so I tore my clothes off and went for a swim. From the water I saw John and Clair sit side by side on the sand. The three of us understood that the years and months of our collective preparations were now all but over. This was a treat – an acknowledgement of all that had passed, and a reconnaissance, to let us both visualize how things might be in the days to come. Now it was a matter of waiting for the conditions, a judgement call with what weather and tide information was available. We would soon execute a series of meticulous and intricate plans, which, in my case, John had long since made.

A week hence the conditions did look just right and so Mother Duck received 'the call'. Twenty-four hours after that, and after more than fifteen hours of swimming she was pulled from the water 3 miles from the French coast. She had missed the second tide and so was being swept, exhausted, back towards the North Sea and away from the headland surrounding Calais. It would be another five hours before the tide would let her make an approach, and by then the gap to the shore would have widened by another few miles given the shape of the coast and direction the tide was taking her. Like most people who made an attempt to swim the Channel, over 90 per cent in fact, she had been beaten by the combination of distance, tide and prevailing conditions. Being Mother Duck she had wanted to carry on regardless. John had no choice but to pull her out for her own safety. The news came back to London via the normal channels – a call from a payphone, somewhere near Dover, probably the Lantern pub, and a subsequent ring-round key people to share the news.

Anna told me, grave-faced, having taken the call from Vicky. I gulped, felt physically sick, and was then instantly engulfed by two conflicting emotions. The first was sorrow, for Mother Duck, or Clair as I thought of her in that moment. No one deserved to make a crossing more than her. No one had done more for the swimmers in the club, as teacher, mentor and proxy parent, than her. She would be heartbroken and on some level I was too. The second emotion was more primal – fear. If she couldn't do it, the chances were that I, aged eleven, would fail too. I tried desperately to block out the emotion, but it wouldn't go away. My swim window would start any day now.

Renata Agondi was a long distance swimmer from Brazil, and a very good one. Rumour had it she had swum large stretches of the Amazon and had a phenomenal capacity for distance, such was her stamina. She had come third in the Capri to Naples race over some 22 miles a few weeks before. She was world class.

On 28 August 1988, days after Mother Duck's aborted attempt, she died, some 5 miles from the French coast, while trying to complete a Channel crossing for the first time. She was fit, experienced, and twenty-five. It was all over the news. The details were unclear but John thought it was hypothermia that killed her. What little inside information was available suggested that she had fallen unconscious on a number of occasions, but that on the final blackout her body just went to sleep for ever. No wonder John kept me awake after a long swim. A tragedy had occurred within the sport of Channel Swimming, but it was not the first. At least three people had died trying to do this, although not all under the supervision of the Channel Swimming Association. They died trying to become one of the successful names on an exclusive list. The French authorities did not see the death of a swimmer in their waters as an inevitable outcome of the 'spirit of adventure' within an extreme sport – a tragic consequence of simple sporting endeavour. They would be launching an inquiry, probably with a view to pressing manslaughter charges. Against whom, no one yet knew, but the rumour was that the coach, pilot and CSA observer who had been in the boat were all potentially in the frame. As my swim window opened and we waited for the weather and the tidal combination to be just right, the tragedy of Renata raised the possibility I might not be allowed to swim at all – part of an emergency response to a preventable death.

The dinner table was silent despite my desire to discuss this news. Mum and Dad said barely anything as we piled into the enormous shepherd's pie John insisted upon. I had an extra-large helping, and some bread and butter on the side. Anna, in her normal way, could read the situation where I could not. After dinner she spoke to me as we cleared the table, and out of earshot. 'Tomsk, this Renata thing has really spooked Mum and Dad. I think they're worried about you having a go. Just so you know. They'll probably want a chat with John about things. I'll keep you posted.'

It seemed a fair point, but not one I was willing to accept. With Clair's failure I was worried, but largely about the distance and the magnitude of the event itself . . . Four years to train for it, and just one day to do it, I reflected. There wouldn't be a second chance before my twelfth birthday in October if I failed, and the season would then be over – too cold, chance gone for ever. So it was all or nothing. And I was not worried about dying. Doctors, medicals and consent were all very well, but also largely irrelevant. The only thing that mattered was John. John Bullet would keep me safe. Of that I had no doubt whatsoever. I remembered his words from the Dutch trip – 'I will always, ALWAYS look after you, Tefal.' I trusted him with my life.

As a wet Atlantic low rained its way across the UK, and with another in its wake, a ridge of high pressure from the south began to reach up and interrupt the conveyor belt, poking up through Biscay and extending defiantly further north. Maybe it would get far enough to reach us, stop, then hang around for a while – a last blast of sunshine and warmth before the long march to Christmas. The moon and sun were approaching the point of equinox and so they would combine to deliver the weakest of neap tides in the days that followed – the lowest possible volume of water into the Channel, and the least tidal effect. I didn't fully understand this at the time, but discovered in later years that John had thought about this in great detail. The trick was to identify the period of least possible tidal influence on any attempt, combined with the warmest temperatures of the year. The run up to the equinox was my best chance.

I went to school at the start of the new term carrying Mum's letter, addressed to the Headmaster and marked 'urgent' in Mum's elegant writing. I pretty much knew what it would say . . . '*Tom is involved with a world record attempt . . . Under normal circumstances we wouldn't dream of pulling him out of school . . . tides and weather dependent . . . short notice window to cross now open . . . Seeking your cooperation in this matter . . . Sorry, Regards, Mary.*'

I handed it to the Headmaster's gowned prefect, went to join my new class, and imagined the face of the Head, Vivian Anthony, as he read it at his desk.

An hour or so later, the same prefect entered the classroom and waited beside the teacher's front desk to indicate a private conversation was needed. Mr Arnold, not one for being interrupted mid-dictation, was walking up and down the lines of desks, reciting from his encyclopaedic memory the events that preceded the downfall of King John. The prefect caught my eye as he scanned the classroom, waiting for Arny to finish his soliloquy. Then followed a quiet word in Arny's ear, a look of astonishment from Arny back to the prefect, and a silent nod to me to pack up my things and leave. This was it then. A now familiar knot, the same one I got when I stood at the water's edge before a big swim, gripped my stomach, and once again, but probably because I was eleven, I wanted to cry. No time for that, though. This was what I *wanted* to do, I told myself.

I waited in the foyer of the main school entrance. Mum arrived in the car but didn't get out, which indicated a sense of urgency. The car door clunked shut and I looked over. Her confident smile and calm exterior were a little too fixed.

'Looks like we're on then, Mum!' I said chirpily, unwilling in my subconscious to show any fear and so trigger her protective instincts. We all had to go through the motions now.

'Yes, looks like it,' she said matter-of-factly as we pulled away from the school gates.

I lay in bed at three in the afternoon, wide awake. The enormous plate of food Mum had brought to my room had been eaten and the plate left empty on the tray. The curtains were closed, but daylight seeped in around the window as my tape player spooled through the *Dirty Dancing* soundtrack on low volume. 'She's Like the Wind' was the only track that remotely seemed to capture my mood, but even that wasn't a very good fit. I lay awake, wishing I could fall asleep.

John's instructions had been simple and clear. Get home, go straight to bed, eat shepherd's pie at about 2 p.m., more sleep, then get up at 9.30 p.m. – no earlier, no later. Once up and dressed, drink some tea, eat a snack and say my goodbyes quickly. He would pick me up at 10 p.m. on the dot, so there was to be no 'fannying around'. Meanwhile, there was nothing else to do. My swim bag had been packed for days, and I was hardly in need of luggage. The clothes I travelled down to Dover in would be good for whatever took place in the next forty-eight hours. I lay in my room alone, thinking. This would be without doubt the hardest thing I might ever choose to do. The sensation of fear mainly came on when I imagined something going wrong: being pulled from the water or having an emotional breakdown during the swim. It was really fear of failure. Better not fail then, I thought. At some point, I fell asleep.

Mum, Dad and Anna stood on the front porch. 'Go Bro,' said Anna gently as she gave me a quick hug. 'Good luck, son,' said Dad as he did the same. 'Take care, Tom-Tom,' Mum said, but in her case there were tears visible, try as I did not to notice them, and the hug lasted a little longer. John stood at the rear passenger door of the blue Vauxhall, holding it open for me. Dennis Wetherly sat in the front seat. John's plan was now in motion.

'Get in, Tefal,' said John, beckoning me onto the back seat, 'and get your head down, lad.'

I looked back at my family. They stood in a tight huddle on the doorstep of our house in the suburban half darkness. I smiled at them from the back seat window, trying desperately to hold my nerve. This was suddenly a massive moment happening in slow motion. It was the moment, I realized, where I could back out and when my family, in numbers, would protect me and my decision. Panic rose up inside me and I reached for the handle of the car door. But then something inside held me back. A quick wave and we were gone.

6. *The Sea of Faith*

3.15 p.m., 6 September 1988 – 10 hours, approximately 4 miles from the English coast, English Channel

Everything went warm. It was blissfully dark and quiet now. The sense of comfort was beautiful. Total peace had arrived. My mind and body experienced a rush of pleasure, just like when I had been given gas and air and an injection when I put a pitchfork through my foot.

But the screaming voices and the thud of the diesel engine snapped me back, violently. I was still in the sea. From darkness to bright light, silence to deafening noise, from warmth to shivering cold, from peace and comfort to piercing pain. I had fallen asleep, only then to wake up. The lurching contrast between the two states was traumatic. I felt immediate despair. Redbeard was on the rail, with Mother Duck and JC – all shouting at me. I must have swum a few strokes in my sleep before eventually slowing to a halt. I coughed some water. Perhaps the intake of sea had triggered a more primitive instinct, to wake up rather than to drown. Dazed but with some sort of adrenaline coursing through me, I looked at the line of faces on the boat. They all read anxiety. JC asked me if I was cold. The doctor was listening. Somewhere in my mind Renata's fate registered and so for the first time on the swim, I lied. 'No,' I replied. Where was that bastard Bullet anyway? This was all his fault, and I hated him. How could he put me through this? He clearly didn't give a toss about me. Where was he?

The blue and white bobble hat was at the prow of the boat,

looking forwards, towards the coast. I saw him there, on his own, and a moment later he turned and looked back at me, raising his arm and pointing behind him as he did so. He was pointing at the cliffs. I looked across to England once again. Some time must have passed before I eventually fell asleep while swimming, because the cliffs were closer than I remembered them. Much closer.

John folded his arms over the rail just beyond the wheelhouse. He stared at me with his trademark half smile and we locked on to each other with our eye contact. Nothing was said. I started to swim again. The pain pulsed through my body. Glancing backwards, I could see the rest of the rail was now clear of spectators. It was just John and me now, finally. The next two or more hours would test every facet of our relationship. If I was to carry on and get to England, I needed him there now, on that rail, and he knew it.

I don't know how or when it had happened, but suddenly John was only just visible, perched at the top of a massive structure. The trawler was no longer a Kentish shore boat built for fishing, but an enormous ocean-going vessel. The steel sides of this ship rose from the sea in a wall of sheer metal, threatening to suck me underneath. At one point the colour of her looming bows changed, from blue to red and then back again. The ship towered over me as I swam alongside. I felt some fear somewhere, on account of being so small yet so close to the huge ship. But there was a sense of awe too. How had I ended up here? Confusion. Disorientation. I needed to see John, so I looked up high into the sky on each breath – trying to crane my neck all the way around to a right angle to see straight up to the sky, so high was this vessel. Then he disappeared in the blinding light of the sun. The bobble hat was nowhere to be found in the glare and the fear took over. Eventually there was a different commotion on board. People were moving around. I glimpsed someone's flesh in the sunlight. Somewhere nearby there was a splash, and I was no longer alone in the sea.

Hallucinations are like those rare dreams you manage not only to remember, but also to feel. They are being awake and asleep at the same time, a set of events that your conscious brain would know not to be real if it were awake, but that feels very real in the moment. And like dreams recalled once awake, you can play them back on demand, like a tape recording, just by thinking about them; each scene stimulating the senses in minute detail. The hallucination took hold for a while in the sea. It is hard to know how long, but more time passed before reality began to claw its way back, assisted by a shock of pain that ran through my legs. I remembered exactly where I was, and how much it hurt. I wanted the hallucination back. It was better than the desperation and the pain. I started to cry, with a rhythm defined by hours and hours of swimming. My wailing was underwater, because the act of drawing breath prevented an audible expression of trauma above the surface. My goggles held more tears than ever before. If I cried until they were full, well, it would all be over. They might pull me out. John might end it for me.

Then I remembered the splash. Who was it? I realized I had been swimming with my eyes closed, so I opened them again.

I saw her legs splashing gently, out in front of me and off to the side I breathed on. I recognized flashes of her powerful front crawl stroke: Mother Duck was in the water with me. She didn't stop and she stayed a few metres away from me. Gradually I pieced it together with what was left of my mental capacity. She was there to bring me home, and I no longer felt quite so alone.

Sometimes just the presence of another cues a surge of emotional release. A couple of years before I would be foul to

Mum when she picked me up from school; upon getting in the car I would become sullen and hostile towards her just when minutes before I was content, and I didn't understand why I did it. The only conclusion was that her very presence triggered a release of pent-up anger and emotion, the source of which was far from clear. This was the same. Mother Duck's presence released my anger, fear and pain. I don't know how long she spent in the water with me. It felt like quite a long time, but time had become relative; I would have traded another two hours of steady swimming from earlier in the crossing for five minutes more of this.

I wanted to share the agony with her, and for her to hear me, and console me, maybe even hug me in the water. But though I could not speak, and we could not touch, having her there ended the sense of total isolation. I needed to unload a tidal wave of anguish on someone. I began to have a conversation with her in my head to bridge the gap of human contact. Mother Duck would understand. She always did, because she was the best of all of us. The young woman who had met me on the poolside with my comedy goggles and doggy-paddle swimming four years earlier, who had seen to my welfare and everyone else's on camp after camp in the Lakes and Dover, who had herself been pulled out of the sea at a similar moment just weeks earlier in a bid to fulfil her dream. Yet here she was, trying to help me to fulfil mine. As another surge of drowsy unconsciousness began to wash over me, I realized how much I needed her there. In fact, had she not been there, or had anyone else on the planet with the exception of Anna been substituted for her in that moment, I believe I would have broken.

As our one-way conversation progressed I finally understood deep inside, although much too late to be of use to me, that what I was doing was not normal. In the final act it had become so utterly unpleasant that I wished it all away. I decided

I would never do this again, ever. Nothing could possibly be worse than this form of mental and physical torture. The thing I thought I wanted for some years now, to hold a world record and be the youngest swimmer, turned out not to be something I wanted at all. Not if it meant going through this. I felt like a little kid who had asked for the wrong Christmas present; pushing and demanding that I got my way, only to unwrap the thing and discover that it was not what I thought it was, and that I had to live with the consequences. 'This will end. This will end,' I began repeating to myself. The darkness slowly came back. As the lights began to dim I noticed John again. The blue and white bobble hat had not moved from his position of over-watch on the rail. The eyes set beneath the hat were boring into me, but almost in pity.

Yet on another level I had been here before. The last hour of that seven and a half hour swim on Windermere that summer, where John had taken the oars himself in the driving rain, his nose dripping with water, eyeballing me silently through the final miles . . . That had been a rehearsal, for now. But even that was scant preparation in the end.

I searched desperately for something else to distract me, a song, a memory or a day-dream, but I had used them all up.

Then I thought, finally, about Anna, Mum and Dad, who I then imagined to be standing on a cliff, scanning the horizon, anxiously looking for their son, of whom they would have had no news. The fact of the matter was that I was still in the water, and still swimming, and they were somewhere in front of me, waiting . . .

'DO YOU WANT TO GO THROUGH THE HARBOUR?' he shouted, as if repeating the question. I didn't remember the conversation starting or understand what the question meant, so I just floated there for a while.

'TEFAL!' commanded John. 'Would you like to swim through the harbour?' he tried again.

This time I looked up and over my left shoulder as I bobbed, confused not to be swimming, unsure of what was occurring around me. The last thing I remembered was thinking about Mum, Dad and Anna, but that seemed a far-off memory. The total and overwhelming exhaustion had almost become analgesia. Things were shutting down. The pain was gently ebbing away, and so too was my ability to swim, to stay afloat. Anything from here would be a matter of remaining conscious and ordering my body to do something it no longer felt able to do. In the near distance to my left I saw the towering grey wall of Dover harbour. We were close enough that the western entrance was visible, but far enough away that the buildings of the promenade were clearly set out behind, unobscured by the wall. For the first time I looked on the imposing concrete barrier from the outside rather than from within. Further away to the left, and set back a few hundred metres, was the English shoreline. The towering white Shakespeare Cliff was lit up by the late afternoon sun that still hovered in the western sky. At their foot the pebbled beach shone out in a thin golden strip.

'TEFAL . . .' implored John. Dr Redbeard was on his shoulder. I looked around in the water for Clair. She was nowhere to be seen. I was on my own again.

'No,' I said, finally answering his question. But it sounded like 'Oh'. My tongue was too swollen to pronounce the word.

'OK, that's fine,' said John immediately. 'Last mile, Tefal. D'ya hear me? LAST MILE!'

I hadn't thought about my reply. I just said something . . . anything. It was an unexpected question, and not one I ever thought I would need to answer. What an odd question. Who cares, and why on earth would you let me decide anyway? Redbeard was there, though, so better to have answered than not.

The thought occupied me for a while. If I had answered 'yes', the boat would have aimed for the western entrance. The ferries would have been held on their giant docks. FE41 would have sought permission from the Harbour Authority to land, citing tides and a tired swimmer as the reason why it must happen. There would have been a tannoy announcement on all the ships explaining the delay. People would have gone up to the rails on a bright September afternoon to witness the moment of completion in slow motion. The promenade would be busy. Pedestrians would gather to observe the landing. Part of me suddenly wished for the attention and regretted my answer. The other part, the part that answered, wanted this ordeal to remain private, hidden, and as uncomplicated as possible.

'One mile' . . . The more I thought about the absurd question, the less would be left to swim. My mind came back into the world for a while, and floated back to a memory . . . Me and Bleachy swam a mile once, on Windermere. That had felt like the hardest thing I would ever do. I was eight. Just three years later and there it was again, one mile. About thirty of them lay behind us, curving an S-shaped trail, bent by the tides, all the way back to France. One mile.

FE41 had vanished. In her place was the tender, low and urgent in the water. On the tender was John, and someone else. I couldn't recall the transition or remember witnessing the process. But it was how things were now and I knew it was real, not a hallucination. John was shouting and repeatedly waving his arm across his body towards the shore in a signal that translated as 'get a move on'. The dull thud of the marine diesel had been replaced by the intense whirring of the outboard. Behind the tender I could now see the western outer edge of Dover harbour, making its way out to sea.

'Four hundred yards!' he shouted. 'Go, Go, GO!' The look

in his eyes was frenzied, unlike any expression I had ever seen him wear. I was sprinting, swimming as fast as I knew how. I struggled to get enough air into my lungs. 'This must end. This MUST END.' Things went dark again.

My left hand felt them first. The smooth rounded touch of the pebbles, underwater at the depth of my extended arm. I opened my eyes and saw them. The stones spinning like a kaleidoscope. I had seen nothing beneath me for hours but the deep and mysterious darkness. Now half of my visual world was replaced by land. I heard them too, rattling and muffled as the late summer waves stroked the shore. Every sense was awake now. I lifted my head above water for air and looked up, gasping. This was England.

I crouched in the water on one knee, placing both hands out to the front to steady me – a track sprinter at the start of a running race. My shoulders and back screamed as I stretched to reach down and avoid toppling over. Both hands touched the seabed. I was anchored now, and the contrast was stark – no longer rising and falling with the ever-turning sea. We had become separate again. My head hung down for a moment, suspended just above the lapping waves on the beach. Salt water dripped off my nose and mouth as I took my first land-supported breaths. I raised my head and looked up.

The beach. I had been here before. We had landed on Shakespeare Beach, at the foot of the cliff and about 200 metres away from the western wall of Dover harbour. This was an isolated place, only accessible via a huge staircase bolted onto the vast cliff face. There were no footpaths that led here.

Three steps. I remembered the three steps. I rose from the water and tried to stand. Instantly I fell back down onto my knees, nearly tumbling sideways into the water. The world was spinning. Three steps and *clear from the water* I remembered. I had to get out of the sea. I tried to stand again and take a step forwards at the same time. My foot landed, so I took another, only to collapse again.

I rose once more with every remaining ounce of energy and started to walk forwards, reminding myself what was required as I went – foot, opposite arm, other foot, other arm. Then I was clear – just pebbles under my numb feet and so I kept going just to be certain, stumbling and knowing it couldn't last. Finally I fell for the last time, back onto my knees, and some metres up the beach. It was over.

Inside there was no euphoria. The moment of acquiring a world record as I had imagined it was, in the event, very different. In my day-dream I stepped out of the water confidently in my Speedos, waving and smiling at the cameras, exchanging hugs with the girl I had the biggest crush on at the time – normally Miss Piggy. And in the day-dream there was a soundtrack playing through the orange foam headphones of my Walkman as I lay in bed: 'Together in Electric Dreams' by the Human League. In the real world, there was no music. No hugs. No smiling. Just me, sitting on the pebbles. I had been through something terrible that had finally ended, and felt only a deep and extreme sense of relief.

Gradually I became aware of a commotion unfolding. I could hear people running on pebbles. I rolled over on the stones, gasping, and slowly sat up, using my arms to raise myself from the ground. I found myself facing back out to sea, to France. A man was running through the waves in his clothes. He looked to be holding a camera. There was shouting. To the left the tender had landed. I breathed out, in, out. About 100 metres offshore was FE41, bobbing silently, her job and that of her crew now done. The sea was serene. Late afternoon sun warmed my skin. I pulled off my goggles, glued to me like suction cups, and as they came away my face felt like an integral part of it had been removed. The world was in clear focus again; the sky was a deep blue and I squinted in the brightness. I felt a hand on my shoulder and Flossie appeared in front of me, yapping in excitement. I glanced up and saw Mum standing above me. She was crying. The hand on my right shoulder was Dad's.

'All right, Mum?' I asked.

'I'm all right, Tom-Tom,' she said through an incredulous smile, wiping away a tear. 'Are *you* all right?'

'I'm all right, Mum,' I said, and looked back out to sea.

John held both of my hands in his. 'Under twelve hours,' he said, looking me in the eye. 'You did it, Tefal.' He was crouching down on the beach to be at eye level as I sat on the stones. He was checking me over, bobble hat still resting on his head. His eyes, though . . . they were smiling and blinking, slightly creased at the outer edges. There was a flicker of emotion, and his voice trembled a little. John held my gaze and we looked at one another in silence. The anger I had felt for him over the previous hours vanished. I had trusted him with my life and together, somehow, we had made it.

I stood on the beach unsteadily, still holding both of John's hands in the way I was used to after a long swim – him the puppeteer, me the giant puppet; Geppetto and a chubby Pinocchio. First lifting me from the ground, onto my feet and into life, and then controlling and guiding me step by step, as a parent does with a toddler. We made our way slowly to the water's edge and onto the tender. FE41 would have to take us to Folkestone harbour in order to land the crew and the boat itself. There would be formalities, and probably a Customs officer. The moment was passing, the adrenaline ebbing, just like the tide. Dr Ian (now my anger had subsided my acceptance of his role had returned) would be curious as to my wellbeing, but that was no longer a problem. I wanted to be with the crew now – with John,

Clair, JC and Spike. Slowly the reality dawned on me, like a joke I had only just understood. I had swum from France to England. There would be a fuss, because on that day, 6 September 1988, I was eleven years and 333 days old. It had taken me eleven hours and fifty-four minutes. I had swum 32 miles because of the tides.

I stopped and looked down the ramp of the launch jetty of Folkestone harbour. Spike held my hand to keep me steady. I didn't remember arriving or what happened on the way – other than Clair's arm around my shoulder as I recovered. They were all there now looking back up towards me, my friends, family and fellow swimmers. Uncle John had held out a loyal hand as the tender landed on the jetty and I stepped ashore. At some point I had been dressed in the tracksuit I was wearing the night before when I left the house. A TV camera crew had arrived and I acted up with an exaggerated look of surprise, which was intended as modesty. The club van was at the top of the slipway, where John was already standing by the open driver's door, waiting. I turned and faced back down the ramp.

'Bye! Thanks for comin', all you lot!' I called out. Anna later told me that my parting line closed the 10 o'clock news.

The campsite outside Dover was quiet, despite the balmy late summer weather. Everyone had gone back to school. Nothing was said, but I understood that this was now a retreat – a rallying point. My family, the club swimmers and the press would be driving back to London. I was to stay in John's care overnight, along with JC – away from all the fuss. I sat in John's own caravan for the first time, and felt safe.

This was John's private place, and despite all the times we camped here, he had always only ever stayed with us in the tents. There were long brown cushions underneath the windows, which I presumed would become my bed. Only I was not allowed to sleep, of course – not yet. I told JC, for John was now attending to other things, that I didn't really feel tired, even though I had not slept since getting up to go to school the day before. He said I was still adjusting to having been in the water for such a long time and so I needed company, but that my body would soon catch up. Then he reached into his pocket.

'Here now, Tom.' He passed me a smart red Swiss Army penknife. It had the logo of the *QEII*, the smartest passenger ship in the world, stencilled beneath the badge. It was a very good penknife indeed. I studied it.

'I went on the *QEII* once – a special trip. Today was a special trip too, and so I want you to have this . . . To say, well done, Tom.' His gravelly voice cracked a little as he spoke.

'Thanks, JC.' I paused, giving him the chance to keep the prized knife, in case he changed his mind.

'You've earned it. That really was one hell of a swim, kid.'

It was a kind gift, of something he treasured. JC rolled out a sleeping bag under the window and found some pillows. The pain, I knew, would come tomorrow. I put the penknife under the cushions of my makeshift bed – the last act I remember from 6 September 1988.

7. *A Whole Army of Little Tefals . . .*

I blushed when Caron Keating and Yvette Fielding, the *Blue Peter* presenters, kissed me for a photo as I sat in between them on the couch. The cameras had stopped rolling but the producer wanted a shot for the 1988 Annual. It was hot under the lights and I was already flushed, half boiled in the blue club sweatshirt John made me wear. I felt myself turning a deep red. I had been given a gold *Blue Peter* badge, the highest award, and asked about my swim. Yvette had pointed out the tan line from my swimming cap, and asked me to re-enact feeding myself tomato soup in the water with the aid of a tonic bottle prop. Behind the cameras John and Anna smirked and made jokes to each other at my expense – safely out of shot and enjoying me going through the terror of live television. The interviews had become easier, though. This was the fifth in three days.

The house was busy. The postman's bag was full every day, mostly with congratulations cards, and the phone rang constantly as I tried to sleep. The occasional reporter appeared outside.

A crate of Heinz tomato soup arrived, with a note from the marketing department to say thanks; I had accidentally mentioned the brand on the news. A random agent from the States called to ask if we would fly out to do some promotional work, like open shopping malls. Dad said no, and I refused the offer of a billboard poster from the soup people on the phone myself.

Poor Anna, meanwhile, had the task of taping all the TV appearances and marshalling all the press cuttings. Members of the extended family got in touch; I had made the CNN morning news, according to Auntie Esther in New Orleans.

Dad's best mate sent a telegram from Zambia saying he had heard it on the World Service. John had ordered me to bed for a couple of days to recover. Things needed to get back to normal, and I needed to get back to school.

'I don't want you getting cocky, Tefal. I won't let you become a big'ead,' John reminded me in the car to the TV studios. John and Dad were both worried about this but Dad had been more circumspect. 'This is phase one,' he said. 'You will be news for a day, but it will die down and get back to normal. Then there will be things you get asked to do for a while – phase two, we will call it – and you should do these with good grace. But at some point this achievement will disappear into the background of your life, and only re-emerge from time to time. That is phrase three. Of all of these, I think phase three will be the best.' And so it was.

The TV appearances were largely done by the Friday after the Tuesday of the swim. When I arrived back from Dover with John, to HQ, the TV cameras were rolling, but John made himself scarce. He never spoke to the media. Reporters scribbled on notepads while TV crews interviewed me, and to my huge pride, Marcus Hooper had been summoned to comment on the breaking of his nine year record. He was kind and generous. He knew, more than anyone, what this meant and how it felt.

I was asked to open a shop on Eltham High Street called Knobs and Knockers, which sold brass fittings. Mum joked as we walked there that I could be the knob and she could be the knockers. I cut the ribbon and grinned at the photographer. They gave me a voucher for £100 of brass gifts to say thank you, so I picked out some things for the next swimming club raffle. On the way home some kids about my age stopped me to ask for an autograph – they had seen *Blue Peter*.

I found myself in Hyde Park, with a Sport Aid VIP badge pinned to my 'Run the World' t-shirt. A man called Bruno

Brookes, who I recognized from *Top of the Pops*, beckoned me onto the massive stage. Bruno introduced me to the crowd as the kid who had just swum the Channel. I in turn introduced Five Star, and watched from the wings as they sang their song. In the VIP area Lionel Blair came over to say hello, but others largely ignored us. Producers and coordinators ran around with clipboards and handheld radios. We were surrounded by pop stars, media and a free bar. We roamed around the chaos, unsupervised and out of place.

When asked to open a private gym in the Docklands I arrived to find that no one knew who I was, or why I was there. Phase three so soon? I thought. A famous actress who I recognized but couldn't name was being eagerly snapped by the press, cutting the ribbon. Lost for something to do, I got changed and did a few lengths in the pool as people milled around drinking champagne. No one spoke to us, so we left – we had a better offer anyway.

That afternoon we headed off to Leyton Orient. The club had sent me free tickets for the Directors' Box. I walked out onto the pitch with my two favourite players, Alan Comfort and Peter Wells, who gave me a ball signed by the whole team. There was a tannoy announcement and I heard clapping from the lightly attended stands. I sat in the players' dressing room before kickoff as Frank Clarke, the manager, issued a plan cum pre-emptive bollocking to the team. We lost 1–3 to Hereford. 'Rise and fall,' Dad said as we left the ground.

Two days later I was in Wales, in the hills above Barmouth Bay in southern Snowdonia for school Outdoor Pursuits week. John was unhappy because I was still on call to be part of the Junior Relay team who were waiting for a tide and weather combination to make an attempt. On the second day, I was out orienteering on the hill and fell awkwardly. My foot swelled up like a balloon and so the Master in Charge, Mr Gardener, drove me at speed to Aberystwyth hospital in his Audi Quattro. I had broken my foot quite badly according to the x-ray, having chipped off a large chunk of bone that was now floating in blood and deciding whether to reattach itself. They set my leg in a cast, placed a giant leather 'Quasimodo' boot over my foot, and gave me a crutch. As she wheeled me out of the hospital the Welsh nurse sang a song that was in the charts, 'A Groovy Kind of Love' by Phil Collins. She had a beautiful voice and sang so we could all hear her. I began to cry.

In 1988, the twenty-first year of his swimming club, John achieved only half of his ambitious list. Clair had not made it on her solo, and the Junior Relay never even left the shore, poor tides and weather cited as the reason. That young team, which took on a reserve in my injury-enforced absence, never got the chance to make an attempt after months of preparation. But as November arrived, I was to be welcomed into an exclusive club at the Annual Channel Swimming Association Awards dinner, as the 333rd and youngest ever swimmer to have made the crossing. Anna and her team mates were there too, honoured for their outstanding two-way relay – a first for the club.

I studied myself in the mirror of my B&B bedroom and let out a long nervous breath. My bowtie was straight and my shirt ironed; my school shoes were polished, and my grey flannel trousers pressed. The hastily sewn-on and newly made blazer badge glinted back at me. I had seen one before, worn by John. The main crest was beautiful. Within the central shield were England on one side, France on the other, the sea in the middle. England's cliffs were recognizable – high and with Dover Castle atop. Where England was in daylight the French cliffs on the other side were in the dark, and instead of a castle, Calais was marked by an enormous radio mast that was transmitting a radio signal, light or both. The contrast of night and day made a point: that Channel Swimming was often measured in hours, rather than minutes. The waves that joined England and France were shared, filling the bottom of the 'V' as if to emphasize the scale of the obstacle. Outside of this centrepiece a mermaid and a merman, for this sport regarded swimmers of both genders equally, faced each other to frame the scene. Together, they held aloft a laurel wreath to symbolize achievement. The gold and black scroll underneath the scene spelled out the name of this peculiar club, 'Channel Swimming Association', of which I was one of the latest members. The badge looked massive in proportion to my chest. Mum and Dad had made sure it was the nicest one, with silver and gold wire. At the bottom were embroidered the words

France to England
1988
Youngest Conqueror

The taxis arrived and the entourage from Eltham made their way to the smartest hotel in Folkestone. The swimming club were dressed up for their moment: Anna and her five team mates, John and JC, Mother Duck, my parents and other families. John's loyal tribe were all present. The confidence and aspiration of Eltham Training and Swimming Club – self-taught, self-funded, and the vision of just one man – had reached a new high-water mark.

I sat next to John as waitresses in black and white uniforms brought plates of food that resembled a Sunday roast, only with smaller portions. We could have been back in the Little Chef, only the setting was grander. John was slightly on edge that night, dignified and polite, but with an undercurrent of defiance. The audience in the large room clapped as speeches were made and awards handed out.

A man called Richard Davey had broken a record for the

fastest crossing from France to England (eight hours five minutes) and received the Rolex watch. Alison Streeter, who I knew of, took the female record for the same thing (eight hours forty-eight minutes). John said he expected her to become the next female two-way swimmer, and I shuddered at the idea of turning around and trying to swim back to France three months earlier. Mike Read, who I liked, having once met him on the beach at Dover with John, retained his title as King of the Channel for the most crossings (twenty-five in all), despite not swimming that year. I marvelled at the idea that anyone would ever consider doing this more than once. A man called Kevin Murphy seemed to be looking to displace Mike as the King, catching up his tally year on year. This was the royal family of Channel Swimming, and I felt slightly out of place.

My swim was eventually announced, but not as a world record. I collected my certificate from the chairman along with a trophy for youngest swimmer of the year. There was a sense of non-acknowledgement that continued throughout the evening.

It explained John's defiant posture. It seemed some people just didn't approve of this type of thing, and therefore of me, or John. I saw for the first time that he was an outsider on the inside – a maverick with his own rule book.

The next morning the blazers reconvened for the Annual General Meeting. John explained that he would be voting against a motion to ban people under the age of twelve from attempting the swim, and that I might wish to do so as well, but that it was my decision. As a successful solo swimmer I was now a member and had voting rights. He told me if I wanted to speak at the meeting, I could.

A sense of crisis pervaded the ballroom. The top table was laid out formally and the atmosphere was one of hushed tension, as if a mighty argument could break out any moment. The French authorities were pursuing manslaughter charges against

Renata Agondi's swimming coach, the pilot of the boat, and potentially the observer from the CSA, though the outcome was not yet known. The authorities both sides of the Channel had expressed grave concern that another life had been lost and wanted immediate safeguards to prevent further tragedy.

The sport of Channel Swimming, pioneered by Captain Matthew Webb, who in 1875 became the first known swimmer, was fighting for its survival. The Channel Swimming Association had been set up to control and promote the endeavour in 1927, when fewer than a dozen swimmers had matched Webb's achievement. Observers, they decreed, would verify claims and validate crossing times, a badge was devised and a committee set up. Although traditional, it was also an internationally facing organization – part of the great British tendency for codification of sport and achievement. But it could not afford another death, especially not that of a child. Sailing and other sea-going pursuits were largely unregulated in the UK, but the fact that swimmers were required to cross the heavily controlled waters of the world's busiest maritime route meant that without the consent of the authorities there would be no sport. To attempt a swim without supervision of the Association was pointless: more dangerous and with no prospect of recognition. In the aftermath of my swim, there was anecdotal evidence of novice coaches and parents pushing kids into the sea in Dover harbour, even throwing stones at them as they stumbled out from the cold. The CSA was being inundated with requests for youth solo attempts for the following 1989 season, mostly from the Indian subcontinent and South Africa. To refuse them all without any reasonable assessment mechanism would be, perhaps fairly, seen as tacit racism. This was 1988, and the blazers had a major problem.

By the time I stood up I already knew it was too late. Successive speakers had made the case for an age ban, initially for anyone under the age of twelve, but to be extended to those under the age of sixteen. There was no logic in passing safety legislation for an eleven year old but not a twelve to fifteen year old. 'A child is a child!' someone had said passionately. I could feel people looking at me for a reaction. 'Calm down,' John had whispered. A reporter in the corner scribbled.

Eventually I rose to my feet, and began an unscripted speech. 'Records were there to be broken' and 'I was proof that age was not a barrier'. I said that 'good coaching was the answer, by people like John Bullet, and there should be other ways to determine the ability of a swimmer . . . Windermere for example' . . . 'And . . .' At that point someone interrupted, shouting that they didn't want a dead kid in the Lake District either. There was no special protection for me in here. Wrong-footed at the interruption, and suddenly aware of being outnumbered, I ran out of words. Stumbling to recover, I looked down at John, who showed me a face of pride before nodding gently at me to sit back down.

A vote was taken. It was all but unanimous. My world record would be locked in for ever. We had lost, and I felt deflated; Marcus had been kind to me, and inspired me, but my chance to do the same for someone else, perhaps another of John's swimmers in years to come, had been taken away. John's face had been unreadable at first, but then, for the first and only time, I saw a hint of sadness in his eyes.

'Rise and fall,' said Dad in the car back to London, 'rise and fall.'

The club Christmas party was at our house that year. Dad had volunteered to host in a spirit of alliance and concordat with John. Anna was in charge of the music, Mum the food, but bar duties, much to Dad's chagrin, were traditionally a matter for John Bullet himself.

'Come to me for your drinks, please,' he said quietly and conspiratorially. I did as I was told, and soon received my first ever brandy and Coke. He held up a finger to his lips as if to emphasize the secret, and winked at me naughtily. The sweetness of the Coke was normal, but the addition of the brandy made me cough when I sipped it, a hot sensation warming my mouth. I felt the effects almost instantly. I went back for another one, and later, another. The next morning I awoke in my bed to a pool of sick. I had been drunk, aged twelve, and was nursing my very first hangover. There was little parental reaction, to the point where I wondered if anyone, apart from Anna, had actually noticed.

I didn't spend much time with John that night, but I knew our relationship had moved on. The drinking was just the latest piece of evidence. We had spent much time in the preceding weeks talking about other challenges, normally while driving to an event where we were asked to be present together, or to check out another young swimmer who had been in touch. Our conversations were changing, as was the balance of power and authority. There was less telling, and more asking. Opinion suddenly came into things. 'Sounding out', Dad would have called it.

John, who was also well known to the British Long Distance Swimming Association, had the idea of a helicopter-supported back-to-back swim of all the major waters of the Lake District. We talked of swimming the Thames, which had only been completed once to anyone's knowledge. Then there was the Irish Sea . . . Loch Ness. All with the old rules: trunks, goggles and a bit of grease. The trauma of 6 September was beginning to fade, and I began to wonder what else we might accomplish together. Other people from the world of swimming had arranged to come to see me swim too. John had seemed almost defensive in these moments, while I was immediately resentful of the people interrupting our world. I hated racing, wasn't very fast, and I didn't want or need another coach. Swimming was about the swimming club, my friends and Anna, but above all else it was about John. I wanted nothing more than was already the case.

As 1989 loomed on the horizon and Christmas Day finally arrived, the family prepared for a magical time. Mum said there were more cards this year, and the one from John was placed in the centre of the mantelpiece, tucked among mine and Anna's accumulated trophies. Around the walls hung mementos from the preceding months, and in a cup given to me by John himself were the hat, goggles and grease-stained Adidas trunks I wore on the crossing.

On Christmas Eve Dad, Anna and I dropped a smart bottle of brandy over to John's small flat in Ladywell Road near the baths. It was the place he had rented for as long as anyone could remember. We left the bottle with his landlady, along with a card Mum had written, and I wondered where he was. Probably working at the pool, or maybe at his caravan. Or maybe he was with the Wetherlies, Cynthia, Dennis and the family – who were very close to John. Perhaps he was with the Kents, Mother Duck's parents. It struck me that maybe we ought to have invited him over for Christmas at ours that year. John had no family to anyone's knowledge, and spent all of his time with us, the members of his club.

It was curious just how little any of us knew about him. Now our relationship was changing I resolved to find out more . . . Where was he from anyway? Where did he grow up? How did he get into swimming? How had he learned what to do and say? I had spent as much time with him in the last two years as with my own family, yet I knew nothing about him really.

'Dad, we should have invited John over for lunch tomorrow,' I said in the car, feeling suddenly guilty for having abandoned him just because it was Christmas. I normally saw John every day of the week – even if I just popped into the pool on the way home from school to say hello.

'You know, maybe you're right!' replied Dad after a pause. 'Ah well, I am sure he will have fun, Tom. And there is always next year.'

The call came about halfway between Boxing Day and New Year's Eve. Anna had answered the phone. Cynthia Wetherly was ringing people to let them know that John was in hospital. The situation was still unclear but it sounded serious. He had had a stroke at the baths, and now a series of them. He was paralysed down the left side and there was a possibility of brain damage. Or even death.

In his hospital bed John lay perfectly still. His eyes were closed and his arms lay symmetrically on top of a thin blanket. Wires and tubes were attached to his nose, hands and arms. His colour was pale. The sterile light in the room, his own room, made everything more sinister. There was a peculiar smell I had learned to associate with hospitals – of bodily things, but not of any one thing in particular. He looked small and diminished in the bed. Machines bleeped to break the silence. The nurse allowed us in in groups of four, to stand at the foot of the bed. As reality confronted each of us, someone ran out in tears. Anna moved to the side of the bed and held John's hand, beginning a one-way conversation. One by one the rest of us added to the dialogue, with awkward statements of no consequence. There was no reply. Eventually, on the orders of the nurse, we left the room. Most of us were crying. Finally came the dark humour. 'Fuck, I wish I could have pretended to be that fast asleep when it was my turn to swim,' offered Rabbit. The gags continued, in a moment of hope.

I got home from school on Tuesday 31 January 1989 and let myself in through the front door. Unusually, I heard Mum's footsteps hurry from the back of the house. She stopped hurrying and froze, standing stock still in the hallway as soon as we made eye contact. She looked at me, with a look that only a mother can muster. She said nothing, but I knew. I fell to the carpet and wept. John was dead.

After five weeks in hospital and a long silent fight to return to the world he had built, John had finally died. The doctors could not understand how he had clung on after so many strokes and haemorrhages. The indications were that he had tried desperately to do so, but, with no communication possible, the people who loved him were unable to share anything of his final journey. Two days before he died I had been to see him again, just Dad, Anna and me. Dad had told us that this was actually about saying goodbye, and that we had to be brave – as brave as we were when we got in the sea to swim – and that John would expect nothing less. He would be proud of us for being just so.

I walked into the same hospital room, alone this time. The room was filled with cards, flowers and mementos. John had changed. All colour had left his face, he had lost lots of weight and his once cannonball frame looked tiny and brittle. A bag of dark urine hung from the bed. The smell of bodily things had grown more acute. The whirring and bleeping of the machines had intensified – now they were simply keeping him alive.

'Hi, John,' I said, breezing in confidently. I heard the note of defiance and deception in my voice, as if masking a fib to my mother. I reminded myself he was not going to reply and a wave of sorrow reared up. I realized this was going to be, aged twelve, the hardest thing I had ever done.

I sat by his side. 'You better wake up, JB, I'm telling you . . .' I whispered, holding his still chubby hand in mine. 'If you don't, I'll have to duff you up,' I said, a smile and a half laugh breaking through the tears. My hand felt some pressure. Gentle at first, but then there it was again. He was squeezing my hand, but he couldn't perform his half of our routine . . . so I did it for him.

'It would take a *whole army* of Little Tefals to duff you up, John,' I said gently, and in reply to myself, while laying my other hand on his dented bald head.

His eyes didn't open, and the squeeze of his hand eventually lessened. The machines continued to whirr and bleep, and his chest continued to rise and fall – the thing he had taught me to look for when confronted with a casualty. I sat there with him in silence for a while. A large lump of spittle had accumulated at the side of his mouth. This would have upset him, so I wiped it away with my finger. I wondered if he was thirsty, but I could not have given him any water, even if he were able to tell me to do so. I realized it was my turn – to give *him* some courage, and to face what was coming. In the way he had given me mine, on the shores of Windermere, and on that beach in France.

Eventually, and wracked with pain, I spoke to him, for the last time.

'John,

'Thank you for teaching me to swim.

'Thank you for teaching me all the other things too, about life. And thank you for the club, and for all my friends.

'Thank you for my world record.

'And, thank you for being my friend.'

Each sentence was slow, deliberate, and punctuated by the need to gasp in a breath, through the tears.

'I will miss you, more than you can possibly know.'

A final gulp of air.

'I love you.'

Holding down a volcano of grief, I summoned myself to let go of his hand, for the last time. Fighting every human desire and instinct, I knew I had to leave him.

'I love you, John,' I said once more, in despair. And then . . .

'Goodbye.'

I stood there looking at him having finally said that word,

our last word. John's left arm twitched slightly. Then, slowly, it moved. He lifted it up, clear of the bed and right up into the air. He held it there for a long moment in defiance, and in acknowledgement of all I had just told him. He was saying goodbye too, and in the only way he could, to me, Tefal, a kid who had come to love him as a father, and with whom he had achieved something truly remarkable. Astonished and somehow glad, I waved my arm back at him, and because he could not see, I said one more thing, loud and clear, so he could hear me.

'Thank you, John. Thank you for ever.' His arm fell back.

I walked out of the hospital room in a dizzying fog of emotion and sorrow, into the grim light of the corridor outside. Dad and the nurse looked at me with pity in their eyes. Dad had tears on his cheeks. 'John held his arm up in the air, to say goodbye, Dad,' I blurted, pleading. The nurse shook her head gently. 'He *did*!' I protested. Then it came; the sluice gate flew open and I wailed hysterically, uncontrollably. Dad threw his arms and whole body around me, cradling me like a baby once again. We rocked gently back and forth. Of what happened next, and until the following day, I have absolutely no recollection.

Epilogue

In the years that followed John's death I drifted slowly but inevitably away from swimming. Others, like me, gradually moved away or did the things the time of their lives demanded. Countless others were traumatized by John's death beyond me, Anna and our parents, particularly the loyal swimming families who had stood by his side over two decades or more. John's impact on so many was hard to truly measure, but his life, and loss, certainly affected the futures of a great many young people, for many of whom he, and his swimming club, symbolized community, ambition and hope.

Anna and many of her friends in the club continued to make things happen, and for a while the girls in particular simply grew the movement. At coaching level, a succession of Senior club members began to fill the void by teaching the things John had taught them; JC, Doug Minde (one of Jon's four successful soloists), Big Steve, Simon 'Tetley' Johnson and Tanya all worked tirelessly to bring through another generation, and to honour John's legacy. They succeeded.

Three years after John's death a team coached by Tetley, and including Anna, made a successful crossing, winning the John Bullet Memorial Trophy, which had been presented to the Channel Swimming Association by the club for the Youngest Relay Swim of the Year. Solo attempts were made and in 1995 Mother Duck, now in her late twenties, finally got across. The long-serving families of the club, like the Wetherlies, Kents, Overies, Waglands and Sinclairs to name but a few, who had been there from the very beginning, maintained a committee structure and funding. Perhaps their real gift was one of continuity, and the gentle stewardship that prevented committed youngsters from becoming otherwise lost. The training lanes stayed busy, and parties were well attended. In later years Tanya in particular made an even greater impact, both by coaching a series of relays and solos, and by staying close to the sport.

But for me those years were an extended wake, often punctuated by teenage misbehaviour and rule-breaking. There were demons alive and within too; at a club disco that I persuaded my school friends to come to on a promise of booze and girls, I buried deep down the shame I felt at what John's reaction would have been to my nipping out for a secret fag.

Salvation arrived in a uniform. The Cadet Squadron at school, just like the swimming club, provided me with a framework where I could achieve new things and learn to play by the rules. Military life began to appeal to me, because, just like long distance swimming, it seemed to be all about empowering the individual and the team, through relentless training, to achieve potentially remarkable things. It also carried with it a sense of excitement, and sometimes danger. Above all, like all those camps at Dover and Windermere, it was enormous fun, spent with others who were on the same adventure. We were often in similarly wild places, in hostile conditions. Swimming, and John, had taught me to cope with such situations – to embrace (and at least try) to enjoy them, but above all to believe that, no matter what happened, I would probably succeed in the end if I tried hard enough.

'Phase three' occasionally came back to visit in some unexpected ways. On the night Frank Bruno won the World Heavyweight title in 1995, I found myself as a guest on the recording of the first episode of *The Frank Skinner Show*. It was an unlikely sofa combination, with Buzz Aldrin and Charlie Kray for company, but that made for some astonishing chats in the green room after the show. For years Dad and I dined out on the moment when Charlie asked Buzz for a signature . . . for his brother. Buzz duly obliged, scribbling 'Dear Ron . . . Best, Buzz' on the back of his Apollo business card, unaware it was destined for one of London's most notorious surviving gangsters. In these moments, John was close; he would have laughed at the facts, before reminding me not to become a 'big'ead'. In future years, through university and my tours of Iraq and Afghanistan with the Army, my one framed photo of John remained part of a small collection of personal possessions and accompanied me on various adventures. And I thought of him often.

More than 300 people came to Falconwood Crematorium for the funeral of John Bullet – a fifty-one-year-old man without a family. The huge cortege blocked the traffic for miles around. A local policeman and father from the swimming club, Tony Parker, saluted John's hearse with a white gloved hand and in full ceremonial uniform as he paused from diverting the traffic at the junction outside John's house. It was a fitting tribute and a final act of respect.

Remarkably, still relatively little is known (to us at least) about John Bullet's early life. At the time of his death, the few personal papers that emerged suggested he was of French origin and of another birth name, and so it seems likely that he was adopted to the UK at some point early in his life to become a Bullet. Anna, Clair and I all recall his being notoriously secretive – sometimes to the point of anger – about the confidentiality he placed on his passport, and so perhaps this was the reason. But between 1967 and 1988 John, a self-taught coach, had built something remarkable. In pure swimming terms, he had achieved fourteen successful Channel relay swims and coached four solos, including three world records – all with kids from the local area. But in reality, he had achieved far more than that. And so in every respect, his funeral wasn't really about swimming at all.

The community he created came out in force to say goodbye. There were swimmers from twenty years ago, whose names were well known to me from their exploits, but whom I had never met. The wider swimming world of South London was also on parade, as were members of the Channel Swimming Association. Parents, children and all-comers jammed into the crematorium chapel. There was a queue of people trying to get into an uninviting and sad place.

Looking back on it now, it was the first time I had truly witnessed the extent of influence he had held on so many others apart from me, Anna and our immediate group of swimmers. As Alison 'Miss Piggy' Wetherly later told me, if you lived in the local area, ever went to Eltham Baths, had a faint interest in swimming, or just read the local papers, you knew about John Bullet.

It had not always been so. In the early years John was simply working for the council as a lifeguard at the nearby pools in Plumstead. He had begun experimenting with coaching, mostly on the sprinting scene, having become involved in various clubs and with the life-saving movement. But once appointed manager at Eltham, he set about building his *own* club, poaching good swimmers to start with, and earning a reputation, before straying into the open water circuit.

He learned as he went, and so the first swimmers like Stephen Wetherly and Marcus, his earliest solo attempts, had it the hardest, even passing out from the cold as John learned how to prepare a swimmer. On his first solo attempt of the Channel, John, the swimmer and crew all fell from the tender in the dark en route to the shore before the start, having come across the Channel themselves on the boat through the night. All of the grease bar one pot was lost overboard. Hours later, a tope shark was seen approaching the swimmer on the crossing before being scared off with cans of beans, used as projectiles.

I was one of many beneficiaries of all those hard-earned lessons of the early years.

But notwithstanding the risk taking, for John swimming was about participation as much as record breaking. He set up a 'B League' of competitive galas for those clubs (which notably included Eltham) whose swimmers were not quick enough to compete at club or county level as sprinters – for how else would they learn or develop?

Despite the mishaps there was an ever-present value: trust. The swimmers and parents alike trusted John implicitly. In speaking to others who fell under his spell, many say the same thing – that he was like a second father; that, as Alison put it, 'he was just always, *always* there for me'. She was with him on the day he had the stroke, working as a lifeguard, and angry that he had made her leave the hydropool at the point where he needed to use chemicals to clean the pool – anxious to protect her from the fumes.

Among the girls, Alison, Clair, Anna and my cousins all offer the same testimony – of his instilling a sense of confidence during some difficult teenage years, and of establishing 'the base', which was wholesome, disciplined, and from which all other things came within reach. A diary entry of Anna's from February 1989 mourns the passing of John, 'the man who gave me my confidence, and so changed my life'.

While the boys were just as devoted to John, the experience they shared was possibly different to the girls'. In every respect John was something of a 'lad', revelling in boyish humour in one moment, but a hard disciplinarian the next. He undoubtedly had his favourites, but overall he was forward thinking for his generation. Most importantly, even now, most of us kids from Eltham would still count on our time with him as the most influential of our formative years, teaching us self-reliance, teamwork and aspiration.

As a coach he was undoubtedly clever – a taker of calculated and controlled risks, and a master of patient psychological persuasion. He was tenacious, fought for his people, and for the things he believed in. In John's self-constructed community all arrived equal; swimming, being part of a team and sharing unity of purpose mattered more than money, the car your dad drove or qualifications. In the days before lottery funding in sport, what you did for yourselves counted; jumble sales, paper runs and discos in the church hall gently shored up the lessons of group-reliance and of 'making things happen' regardless. John had many faults too, impatience, stubbornness and irascibility among them, but they were outweighed by kindness, humour and, in his own unique way, love.

John never received a penny for his services (other than for his job running Eltham Baths) – nor did he expect to. In the modern era he could have been a contender for the Sports Personality Unsung Hero award, provided he didn't upset too many people along the way. But when I think about John and his legacy thirty years on, the question for us today might be whether our risk-aware era would even tolerate an amateur organization pushing the boundaries of youth endeavour in the way he did. I wonder if he would have been celebrated or censured, and, suspecting the latter, I can't help feel that we have lost something. Maybe we need to relearn the maxim that reward and achievement requires risk, and that in encouraging our children to fulfil their dreams, we need to trust in others. We cannot do it alone.

No memorial exists to the extraordinary achievements and legacy of John Edward Bullet. But for generations of Eltham children, he was simply unique. He taught us that anything is possible, but especially when you have some tomato soup, a pot of grease and an 80s mixtape to hand.

Acknowledgements

This book is largely a tribute to John Bullet and his many accomplishments. But the book, like the events it describes, would never have been possible without the help of others, to all of whom I am deeply indebted both then and now. Many of the families, friends and characters of those times are not referenced as much as perhaps I would have liked. I hope this is to no one's lasting distress, not least since I have tried to represent faithfully the events of those years as they appeared to me at the time, and to include those who were there as much as possible. To all who made a contribution to Eltham Training and Swimming Club, The Channel Swimming Association, and surrounding organisations in whatever form, especially the loyal swimming families and friends from 'back in the day', please accept collective thanks for the roles that you played in our real-life script, and please also accept my own apologies for not having been able to include you all personally. Without you there would be no events to describe, and no history to salvage.

In writing the book I have found the support and counsel of Alison and Stephen Wetherly, Clair Kent and Marcus Hooper invaluable. Our experiences were shared yet different, and I hope that your perspectives and contributions are faithfully represented.

As a first-time author I am also indebted to some of the wonderful people one meets on the journey. To an old pal, Sarah Maclay (nee Ritherdon), for knowing what to do and who to call in the first place; to Jim Gill for hearing it out, sharing cricket yarns and making it happen; and especially to Helen

Conford, my editor, for being wise, kind and patient – I have learned so much. Thanks also to my copy-editor Tamsin Shelton and to the wider Penguin team; in particular to Margaret Stead and Annabel Huxley for the final months, and also to Ingrid Matts, Rebecca Lee and Shoaib Rokadiya for their contribution.

To Hugo and Cat Morris at Deloitte for supporting this venture in a heartbeat, and to Chris Recchia for the same – I am very lucky to work for genuinely good people. To Tom Hollander and Hannah Pescod at Bandstand for dusting me down and offering a bit of encouragement when I needed it. And to Owen Amos for writing an article, out of nowhere, for BBC online which triggered the whole thing. As a book drafted entirely on the daily commute to Waterloo over a twelve-month period, a nod also to South West Trains for all the delays which kept the project broadly on track.

To Mum and Dad. You are true role models. Your love, wisdom, humour and tolerance have never faltered, and those are the foundations which make everything possible.

To my lovely Helen; for backing me when I doubted myself, and for the unflinching support, love and understanding that makes our family.

Finally, to Anna 'the Moog', my cherished big sister. From the day we walked into Eltham Baths together as small children in 1985, to the monster-essay-crisis that produced this book over thirty years on, you were there. Thanks for all the shared memories and the ones yet to be written. You are the brightest star in my sky, and, for the record, a pretty good swimmer.